David Jones

Writer and Artist

By the same author

W.B. Yeats: The Man and the Milieu
Making of George Orwell
Eliot's "Four Quartets"
Visual Imagination of DH Lawrence

David Jones
Writer and Artist

Keith Alldritt

CONSTABLE • LONDON

Constable & Robinson Ltd
3 The Lanchesters
162 Fulham Palace Road
London W6 9ER
www.constablerobinson.com

First published in the UK by Constable,
an imprint of Constable & Robinson Ltd 2003

A copy of the British Library Cataloguing in
Publication Data is available from the British Library

ISBN 1-84119-379-8

Printed and bound in the EU

Contents

Preface

This is the first formal and complete biography of the painter-poet, David Jones, although other books have been published that contain a great deal of information about his life. Three of these books are of special importance. *Dai Greatcoat*, published in 1980, is a biography in the form of letters that David Jones wrote to four close friends, one of them being René Hague, who edited the book and supplied an introduction and some linking narrative. *The Long Conversation*, which appeared in 1981, is a memoir of David by a Canadian scholar, William Blissett, who visited him from time to time between 1959 and David's death in 1974. It gives a vivid and detailed picture of David in his last year and contains David's own memories of and anecdotes about his earlier years. *David Jones – The Maker Unmade* by Jonathan Miles and Derek Shiel, which was published in 1995, is primarily a thoroughgoing account of David's career and achievements in the visual arts. But it is based on very extensive research into David's life and gives a great deal of information about it. To these three works, as the footnotes indeed show, the author of this biography is much indebted.

The first biography of a subject is inevitably different in its aims from any that will come after it. Later ones will often offer additional information and new perspectives. A first biography, and this is particularly true of this one, will have a campaigning purpose to it: a case has to be made for the interest and the importance of the subject. Moreover, as the period of high modernism in literature in English, that began in the 1910s and came to an end in the 1950s, continues to recede from us and is no longer fashionable, it seems necessary to assert the critical claims for two of the great works belonging to that literary movement: David Jones' *In Parenthesis* of 1937 and *The Anathemata* of 1952. To know the biographical circumstances in which these two long poems were completed leads to an increased respect for them. I have been less concerned in this biography, therefore, to supply a lot of biographical detail than to tell the story of how a life that contained much pain and suffering was redeemed by enduring achievements in literature and in painting.

Throughout the biography I refer to my subject as David. When I first began writing the book I referred to him as Jones and then as David Jones, but neither seemed quite right. A few years ago I wrote in the Preface to my biography of Basil Bunting (a great admirer of David Jones) that 'I have taken the decision to refer to my subject as Basil throughout this biography. He was a man who, as he said, liked people with no side on them. And this showed in his attitude to names. Very soon after I first met him in 1970 he was Basil to me as to everyone else whom I knew that knew him. It seems right and proper to refer to him in this way as I attempt to tell the story of his life'. I never met David Jones, but as I have increased my understanding of him in my research and writing I sensed that his attitude in this matter was similar to that of Basil Bunting. So David it is.

As I have worked on this book I have been the recipient of countless kindnesses and generosities. My greatest debt of gratitude is to my kinsman Robert Alldritt and his wife Joy. Entirely unpaid they have spent many hours and travelled many miles to find the evidence on which much of this book is based. They have obtained marriage certificates, birth certificates, they have unearthed church records and long-forgotten parish magazines. They have engaged in worldwide correspondence with people remotely related to David Jones and his forebears, they have been ready to assist with anything and everything that I found problematical. The contribution of Bob and Joy to this book has been immense.

I must also thank their friend and mine, Maureen Piper, for her steady assistance that has continued throughout the period of writing. Regularly she has sent me materials that have shed light upon certain periods and certain persons in David's life. Her skills as a genealogist have been invaluable.

I am also indebted to Rosemary Grayston for many helpful conversations about David Jones. Rosemary accompanied me to Salies-de-Béarn, where she contributed energetically to the research, and to Capel-y-ffin, where she saved me from missing a major piece of evidence.

Janet Fletcher has typed the manuscript with great care and efficiency. I am very grateful to her for the interest she has taken in it, for her many insights into the subject and her suggestions for improvements in the writing.

Finally I would like to express my thanks to the literary executors of David Jones's estate and to Messrs Faber and Faber for their kind permission to quote from David Jones's work.

Illustrations

1

Family, Childhood and Youth 1895–1909

HIS ANCESTRY WAS A matter of great importance to David Jones, both as a man and as an artist. The heritages which were passed on from his father and from his mother were quite distinctive and contrasting. His forebears on his father's side lived in Flint in North Wales and were Welsh-speaking. David's father's father was born at Ysceifiog, and as a young man he set up a workshop and small business in nearby Holywell where he was known as Jones Plasterer. In that same small country town David's father, James Jones, who was born in 1860, was apprenticed to a printer. He then went to work in the print-room of the local newspaper, the *Flintshire Observer*. The family appears to have lived in fairly humble circumstances. The census of 1881 records his older sister's occupation as that of lady's maid. James Jones subsequently left Wales and found work in Liverpool. In the mid-1880s James Jones moved to London to work on the printing staff of the Christian Herald Publishing Company. He began as a compositor, then was promoted to the position of printers' overseer and finally became production manager. David would sometimes visit his father's printing office at the *Christian Herald* and was fascinated to see how the blocks for illustrations and advertisements were engraved on boxwood in reverse. It was a technique that he himself would employ in later years.

David Jones knew that his father felt extremely Welsh. But the family in Holywell had been Church of England and thus incurred 'the suspicion which in my father's day fell upon the Church of England in Wales, that of being on the whole an anglicizing agency – and that in spite of many an "old vicar" of rooted and passionate Welshness who knew of Dafydd ap Gwilym as well as Wordsworth and Horace.'[1] James Jones' parents had been determined that their son should be as English as possible, for this was the way to have a successful career; to use the Welsh language was a handicap. The consequences of his parents' attitude was that James was cut off from the culture that encompassed such great poets as Dafydd ap Gwilym. His rather feeble grasp of the Welsh language was a pain and a sadness for him, feelings which his son David came very much to share.

In 1888 James Jones married above himself when he became the husband of Alice Ann Bradshaw. He was an emigrant artisan; she was the daughter of a Thamesside mast-maker and her family had a degree of middle-class standing and refinement.

David Jones was to devote a lifetime to the study of Wales and of Welsh culture, largely as a result of his love for his father and his feelings for the culture that had been lost to him. But the cultural inheritance he derived from his Rotherhithe mother is similarly prominent in his work. *The Anathemata*, for instance, is in places a hymn to London and one of the several voices speaking in the work is that of his maternal grandfather, Ebenezer Bradshaw, who declaims over several pages an unshakeable commitment to probity, professional standards and fair dealing. He died before David was born, but from listening to the many memories of his mother and his grandmother David knew him to have been a forceful personality who read the Book of Common Prayer, the Bible and poetry by Milton every morning before having breakfast with his wife. Ebenezer would then set off for his riverside workshop where he would do his accounting and supervise the working of timber imported from distant places such as Norway, the Indies and Oregon. He was a man of many and firm principles, and proud that the name of 'Bradshaw' was the first one on the warrant that brought King Charles I to his execution. He even claimed, without any supporting evidence, to be descended from Justice Bradshaw, the regicide. He was also proud to serve as parish clerk at St Mary's, Rotherhithe.

It was in this eighteenth-century church of yellow brick that on 2 September 1853 Ebenezer Bradshaw married Ann Elizabeth Mockford, the daughter of a Rotherhithe boat-builder. David Jones's memories of his maternal grandmother were of an old lady but he could easily picture her as a young woman when she had been known as 'the beautiful Miss Mockford'. She was reported to be of partly Italian descent and there is some evidence to suggest that she was related to the Protti family of Milan. She had, David remembered, the 'symmetric features and what I believe is called an "olive complexion" and very dark eyes, such as we tend to associate with the Middle Sea . . .'[2] He remembered well her dislike of the English winter and in one of the notes in *The Anathemata* he recalled how she was saddened when the cries of the lavender-sellers began to be heard on the streets of Rotherhithe, for this meant that summer was almost gone.

Three years after her marriage to Eb Bradshaw Ann

Elizabeth gave birth to her daughter Alice Ann, the mother of David Jones. Eb was apparently able to give his daughter an education, for in the census of 1871 her occupation is recorded as that of pupil teacher. In an autobiographical essay David remarked that his mother had drawn well as a young woman: her drawings 'were in the manner of the Victorian drawing-master; not only competently but delicately and sensitively drawn . . .'[3] One of David's earliest memories was of three of her drawings: 'one of Tintern Abbey, another of a Donkey's Head, and a third of a Gladiator with curly hair'.[4] David also noted that she had given up the practice of her art long before he was born. She once told him that 'when one gets married there's no time for such things as drawing'. Perhaps such a genteel activity was not suited to life with the none too prosperous young Welsh printer. Certainly James Jones had no home of his own to which he could take his bride. The census of 1891 shows them still living, three years after their marriage, in the home of Alice's parents, Ebenezer and Ann Bradshaw. The address was given as 11 Princes Street, Rotherhithe, Southwark, but is no longer to be found on current maps of the area.

James and Alice Jones had their first child, a son, in 1889. At his baptism he was given the names Harold Thomas Peart, the latter being a family name. Less than two years later the couple had a daughter, Alice Mary. Four and a half years later, on the evening of All Saints day, 1 November 1895, David Jones was born. He was given the middle name of Walter. In later life, when he became a Catholic, David would drop this second name and replace it with Michael. On a voter's list at the end of the 1930s, for instance, he appears as Jones, David Michael.

By the time of David's birth his family were living at 67 Arabin Road, Brockley, which was nominally in Kent, but in actuality part of the suburban sprawl of Greater London. Brockley is now a part of Lewisham and the house and street in which David was born are very much like those described by H. G. Wells in his novel about genteel working-class aspirations at the end of the nineteenth century, *Love and Mr Lewisham*.

The 1901 Census reports that seven people lived at 67 Arabin Road at that time. There were the two parents, James and Alice Jones, and the three children: Harold aged eleven, Alice aged nine, and David aged five. The children's grandmother Ann Bradshaw, now a seventy-two-year-old widow also lived with them, as did a lodger, an eighteen-year-old Welshman, William Randall, who gave his occupation as civil servant with the Education Board. Number 67 was a small house at the end of a long row of terraces. Still standing, the house, which was built in 1900, has a tiny front garden, a narrow path and a front bay window ornamented with two white Corinthian columns. Upstairs at the front there are two bedroom windows. Next door in David's childhood there lived a greengrocer who was a street trader. He stabled his horse in the back garden.

For the Jones family of five the house had very limited space and when David was still a child they moved a few yards away to 128 Howson Road, a corner site at the junction with Dalrymple Road. This was a larger house in another street of working-class houses quite close to the tracks of the London and South Coast Railway. David's future fiancée, Petra Gill, described his parents as 'humble and ordinary with a pinch of Cockney in their speech'.[5]

Yet despite the rather ugly and straitened suburban setting in which they lived, David and his brother and sister grew up in a family environment that had strong cultural aspirations. Religion was also a powerful force in their home, and was much discussed there as mother and father adhered to different wings of the Church of England. Their mother was sympathetic to the High Church and to the beliefs of the Victorian theologian Edward Pusey, a leader of the Oxford Movement. Their father was Evangelical and belonged to the Low Church. Such a difference may well have been a source of tension in the family for in the parish of Hatcham, of which Brockley is a part, parishioners at that time took their churchmanship with intense, even combative seriousness. Less than ten years before the Jones family settled in Brockley Evangelical members of the congregation of the parish church of St James' had rioted against their high church, 'ritualist' Puseyite vicar and clergy. Here is how the historian of St James's, the church in which David was baptized on 2 February 1896, described the situation:

The period between 1868 and 1885 was a time of controversy and great bitterness among church people. This conflict between vicar and people gave St. James a nationwide notoriety . . . An extracts book held in the church archives consists of more than a hundred cuttings from over 20 periodicals, four local papers and 14 national publications. St. James' parish owes these extracts, which show the exciting struggle in which the majority of the congregation were involved during that controversial period, to Mr. H. W. Saunders, the People's Warden, who led the congregation against the clergy of the parish. This battle included fights in church, prosecutions for assault, incessant arguments and incense thrown about the streets.

One particular Eastertide, when things had become particularly unpleasant, the local division of the Metropolitan Police had to arrange for several men to perform special duties on Good Friday. St. James's was described as a 'Bear Garden' and Police Constable 162P West was ordered to clear the church. The clergy made their way out to unseemly cheers, hisses and groans. During that Bank Holiday the parish was out in force, shouting and screaming.[6]

Such was the Evangelical fervour in the parish in which the Jones children grew up. They attended Sunday school very regularly, and the parish magazine for May 1908, some six months before David entered his teens, lists all three of them as winners of prizes.

Their father James Jones was also a lay reader at St George's, the small Victorian, red-brick church in Foxtree Lane, Brockley, until 1893 a mission house to St James's. This fervent Evangelical was upset and angered to discover that at the early age of seven David had High Church leanings. The incident that so angered James Jones demonstrates very clearly two important features of David's singular mind and sensibility: his deep and delicate feelings for the spiritual and his love of rite and ritual. The episode which remained forever in David's memory occurred on a Good Friday. David was alone at home and went into his father's well-tended garden that had flower beds edged with low fences made of slats of light wood. David was moved on that solemn day of the Christian year to break off two of the slats to make a cross. He went into the greenhouse to find a nail to fix them together. In so doing he knocked down and smashed some earthenware flowerpots. He then paraded about the garden, holding aloft his cross. His father suddenly appeared, returning from a church service, and was appalled at what he saw. The damaged garden and the ritualistic behaviour of his son made him white with anger.

As a child in church David was inclined to kneel during

the reciting of the creed. Even his mother with her Anglo-Catholic sympathies was embarrassed to see this in an Evangelical church such as St George's. She herself retained the intense religious devotion she had learned from her father, the mast-maker. She sang to her children a great deal, and was often heard to be singing:

> Alice Bradshaw is my name
> Simple is my station
> Rotherhithe is my dwelling place
> And Christ my salvation.

Alice also sang music-hall songs to her children. The first that David remembered hearing was a patriotic ballad celebrating General Charles Napier's exploits in the Baltic theatre of the Crimean War:

> We'll go to the Baltic with Charles Napier
> And help him to govern the Great Russian Bear.

This war would have had a special interest for Alice in that, as David records in the Preface to *The Anathemata*, her uncle William had 'served in the ranks in the Crimea'.

David's earliest memory also had to do with a military occasion, one that had occurred during the Boer War at the very end of the Victorian period. Sound asleep in his cot beside his mother's bed in the house in Arabin Street, he was suddenly awakened by the sound of marching soldiers and an army band. Then to his great joy there came an 'equestrian column and the inimitable sound of steel-shod horse hooves, and the sight of white dust rising, and the metallic sound of bugles'. The soldiers who so impressed the small boy turned out to be a detachment of the City Imperial Volunteers, who were parading through Brockley and other nearby suburbs in order to promote recruitment for the war going on in South Africa.

If this earliest memory initiated David's lifelong interest in soldiering, another very early memory confirmed a love that stayed with him forever, his love of Wales. In a letter to Saunders Lewis in 1971 he spoke of 'this passionate conviction that I belonged to my father's nation that I certainly felt by the time I was seven . . .'[7] He was seven in 1902 but the memorable moment of solemn realization of his involvement with Wales was dated in an autobiographical essay as some two years later, 'in 1904 or thereabouts'. The occasion was his very first visit to Wales and his first meeting with members of his father's family. He was greatly taken by the landscape and the seascape of the area of North Wales in which his father had grown up. Seeing Arfon and Gwynedd Wen 'with the taut sea-horizon' was such a powerful experience that he felt that 'a Rubicon had been crossed'. This initial visit, he continues in the same essay, 'made an indelible mark not to be erased'.[8]

This crucial first journey to Wales involved people as well as landscape. David especially remembered meeting his paternal grandfather, John Jones, the plasterer. David's enduring first image of his father's father was of a 'tall, powerful man . . . seated near the little stone oratory of St. Trillo on the sea-shore above the wattled sea-weir that was in those days still in use in Rhos and the vicar of Landrillo was still entitled to his tithe of fish from that weir'. This was the first of many 'happy visits to my relatives in North Wales'.[9]

Back at home in suburban London the young David tried hard to stay in touch with his Welsh heritage. When his father sang in Welsh songs such as *Mae hen wlad fy* and *Ar hyd y nos*, David would attempt to imitate him. But unsuccessfully. As a writer David would employ sound most effectively, yet singing never came easily to him. More helpful and sustaining to his intense interest in Wales was his close perusal of two or three thirteenth-century drawings of Welsh foot-soldiers reproduced in J. R. Green's *Short History of the English People*. Years later he recalled that 'These were a particular delight to me. And what lively drawings they in fact are. The draughtsman undoubtedly got the Welsh "look"'[10] His Welsh patriotism was so intense that when he was taken to Westminster Abbey as a boy he spat on the tomb of King Edward I as an act of protest against the conquest of Wales by that Plantagenet monarch.

Books to do with Wales were a delight to him throughout his boyhood. He read George Borrow's *Wild Wales*, Lady Charlotte Guest's translation of the *Mabinogion,* and Sir Richard Colt-Hoare's translation of the twelfth-century chronicler of Wales, Giraldus Cambrensis. Even at the end of his life David continued to take pleasure in such books. A year before he died he told Saunders Lewis, 'I still have Rhys and Jones' *The Welsh People* given me as a birthday present by my father in 1911 and O. M. Edwards' *Wales* (in the Story of the Nations series) round about the same time; and long before that my sister used to read to me children's versions of the tales of Malory – because I was *very* late in being able to read.'[11]

This was one of several occasions on which David Jones spoke of his backwardness at reading during his childhood and his reliance on his sister Alice, more than four years older, to read to him. In the poem 'The Tutelar of the Place' there is a passage evoking a memory of a brother and a sister playing together. It suggests that the relationship between David and Alice was a close one:

Cheek by chin at the childer-crock where the quick tears drop
and the quick laughter dries the tears, within the rim of the shared
curd-cup each fore-reads the world-storm.
Till the spoil-sport gammers sigh:
                                             Now come on now little
children, come on now it's past the hour. Sun's to roost, brood's
in pent, dusk-star tops mound, lupa sniffs the lode-damps for
stragglers late to byre
Come now it's time to come now for tarry awhile and slow
                              cot's best for yeanlings
                              crib's best for babes
here's a rush to light you to bed
here's a fleece to cover your head
against the world-storm
          brother by sister
under one *brethyn*
kith of the kin warmed at the one hearth-flame[12]

Brother and sister would also organize concerts together:
at one of these gatherings Alice played the piano and David
recited passages from Shakespeare's *Henry V*; there was
also 'A Grand Torchlight Procession' in which David appeared as Cadwal, an ancient Briton, and Alice as Britannia.
David recalled a number of occasions when he would pay
Alice to read to him: a particular favourite of his was a
paper-covered series called *Books for the Bairns*. He especially enjoyed the one that dealt with King Arthur's knights,
the story entitled the 'Knight of the Sparrowhawk' being
one that long remained vivid in his memory. Another great
pleasure to him was Macaulay's *Lays at Ancient Rome*.
During his childhood his interest in history grew very
strong. He walked all the way from Brockley to Greenwich
to see ' Nelson's relics' and he would go to the Tower of
London to study the large collection of armour there.

In that very religious home he also came upon volumes of theology, one of these being *The Christian Year* by the Anglican theologian, John Keble. The illustrations in this book captured David's attention. They were by Johann Friedrich Overbeck, a prominent member of the Nazarenes, a group of German artists who were a model for the founding members of the British Pre-Raphaelite school.

While still a child, David's interest in and understanding of the art he encountered was very advanced, as was his ability to draw. Indeed, in using this latter skill he showed a considerable degree of precocity. However, in the three Rs he continued to find himself painfully behind and the feeling was aggravated by the dawning realization that he could not forever inveigle or pay his sister to read aloud to him. At the same small dame school in Brockley run by two young women to which his father sent him, he strove and strove to learn to read to 'make those lines of black things mean something to me'.[13] At last he did – as if by magic.

Throughout his life there would appear women with whom David would fall deeply in love and who would be an inspiration to him. The first of these muses was the younger of the two ladies who ran the Dame school. Very late in life he could still remember that she had 'two long plaits of peat-dark hair, a very white skin and a smile that was bewitching'. He hastened to school every morning to discover what she 'might be able to effect'. And finally she managed to overcome his reading block. There is a suggestion of Ovidian transformation in his later account of this moment. 'Was it by enchantment? . . . I don't know, but by whatever craft, at least some measure of the metamorphosis was achieved, in that the printed page began to mean something.'[14] But even the mysterious powers of his muse could not help the young David in his struggle with mathematics. This was a subject in which he was completely uncomprehending. He later explained this difficulty by saying: 'I could not relate the concrete, tangible and desirable with the formal and conceptual.'[15]

After some months at the small dame school, David moved on to the nearby state school, Brockley Road School. A red-brick Victorian building, it had between three and four hundred pupils and sixteen teachers (eight men and eight women) under the headmaster, Mr Garside. In his published writings David Jones never mentioned his time at this school. It seems likely that he took little interest in conventional schooling, although he did win a book, *Birds I Have Known*, as a school prize for grammar in the summer of 1907 when he was eleven. But the only subject that really appealed to him was drawing. This was an activity that had naturally and easily come to him from the age of five onwards. He once wrote that 'To attempt to convey on paper this or that object seemed to me as natural a desire as, say, stroking a cat, and I couldn't understand why my brother and sister had not the same compulsion.'[16]

Animals were his usual subjects for drawing. His parents would take him to London Zoo and afterwards he would do drawings and watercolours of the animals he had seen there. An especially impressive drawing is 'The Lion', which he never offered for sale, retaining it until his death. Another powerful drawing is of a dancing bear drawn at a bedroom window in 1902, when he was seven. This also remained a favourite among his drawing until the end of his life; it was of one of the brown bears that were paraded around the streets of Edwardian London and made to dance by their keepers, who hoped for coins from passers-by. The pavement artist was another of the familiar mendicants in the society of that time. David recorded that his mother, seeing his artistic talents develop, feared that he might one day be reduced to that kind of beggary.

But early on he achieved success. It was presumably one of his teachers who showed his work to officials of the Royal Drawing Society in Queen Anne's Gate. And here, when he was still a boy, his drawings were first placed on public exhibition. But despite this recognition David later came to believe that as he entered his teens he gradually lost the freshness of his earlier, childhood perceptions. To Robin Ironside, who in 1949 published the first anthology and account of his drawings and paintings, he recalled his sense that those pristine perceptions had been dimmed by the models to which with the coming of adolescence he began to look: 'illustrations in boys' magazines', 'illustrations to old Royal Academy catalogues' and 'the general dead weight of outside opinion'.[17] In spite of this loss in vision, very reminiscent of that described in Wordsworth's ode 'Intimations of Immortality', David was never uncertain about what was his calling. There was, he told Ironside, 'no doubt about the artistic vocation'.

It must have been this certitude that made him fret about continuing to attend Brockley Road School. Early in his boyhood he had made up his mind that 'I wanted only to pursue the practice of the visual arts and go to an art school.'[18] He admits that he nagged his parents about this until finally they gave way. They allowed him to apply to Camberwell School of Art perhaps partly because its prospectus declared that the School's policy was not just to instruct in the practice of the fine arts but 'to provide instruction in those branches of design and manipulation which bear on the more artistic crafts and trades'. This must have eased his parents' anxieties, particularly his mother's, about the artistic young David's ability to support himself and not end up in penury. Even so, his extreme youth must have been a cause for anxiety on their part. In 1909, when he became a student at the nearby Camberwell Art School, he was only fourteen years old. Among the male students he was the only one still wearing short trousers.

2

At the Camberwell School of Art 1909–14

THE CAMBERWELL SCHOOL OF Art and Crafts was one of the more prominent and flamboyant buildings of south London. It was quite new, having been erected in 1897, two years after David was born. It was brick with heavy stone facings in the baroque style. A large and imposing pile, it had grand rounded pediments, draped with statues, tall chimneys, a cupola and broad classical pilasters supporting the entrance porch. In the long room where the art design class did their work was a stained glass window honouring the Pre-Raphaelite painter Ford Madox Brown. Along with art design the School offered instruction in lettering, illuminating and book illustration. There was also, unusually for an art school, an English literature class in which the plays of Shakespeare, lyric poetry, ballads and Coleridge and Chaucer were taught. They would all become important references in the work of the future writer.

David Jones in his knickerbockers and Eton collar spent his first months at Camberwell developing his skills at drawing plaster casts of sculptures from classical antiquity. Only later was he permitted to join the class drawing from life. The college authorities were reluctant to allow such a very young student to look upon and draw models posing in the nude. The many plaster casts he drew included Michelangelo's *David*, a Donatello and the Greek piece, *Boy With a Goose*. Two casts especially interested him and remained in his memory. And each was related to a later preoccupation: the first contributed to his lifelong consideration of the nature of the feminine – this was the *Venus of Milos* which he thought most 'gracious' and 'a marvel of serene beauty'; the second was *The Dying Gaul*, a cast of a Roman marble copy of a bronze erected at Pergamon by an ally of Rome, King Attalos I, to celebrate an imperial victory over a group of Celts who were resisting Roman control of Asia Minor in the third century BC. Late in his life, in an essay entitled 'The Dying Gaul', David Jones explained his instant sympathy, as a very young man, for this figure with his 'typical oblong Celtic shield and his torque' or ornamental metal collar. In his early years at Camberwell David's knowledge of Celticism was not extensive but in contemplating this figure he sensed something that was particular to the Celts, and especially to the Welsh with whom he so strongly identified. Many years later when he knew far more about the Celts and about the history of Wales, he recalled how his first acquaintance with *The Dying Gaul* had conveyed to him 'a continuity of struggle and a continuity of loss'.[1]

David's susceptibility to loss, sadness and melancholy must have been greatly intensified at the end of his first year in art school. For in November 1910 his brother Harold fell ill and died in the house at 128 Howson Road at the age of twenty-one from pulmonary tuberculosis. Harold had worked as an advertising clerk. The death certificate records that James Jones, Harold's father, was present at his son's death. The parish magazine of St James's Church, which the family attended regularly, noted his death 'after an illness which was most patiently borne' and went on to say that 'Young in years, but ripe in Christian experience, his sincere wish at the last was to be *"with Jesus"*. The testimony of his last few days must have robbed death of its sting and will remain fresh in the memory of those he has left behind.' During these last days David was sent to stay with an uncle 'a rather grand old Gladstonian Liberal', who lived 'on the south coast in an old fortress or gun emplacement converted into a house – right on the shore, the sea spray hit the windows'.[2] This uncle, his mother's brother, made him memorize passages from Macaulay's *Lays of Ancient Rome* and recite them to him at bedtime.

In his critical study of David Jones, Thomas Dilworth speaks of 'an increase in his mother's affection for the fifteen-year-old David' after the devastating loss of his brother, and suggests that the teenage boy's response to this surge of love from his mother entailed 'the repression of sexual feelings'.[3] Dilworth sees this as an important factor in the development of the neurosis which lasted throughout David's life, on occasion causing nervous breakdowns and, in 1947, when he was fifty-one, inducing him to undergo six months of Freudian psychoanalysis.

The unhappiness and emotional upset of November 1910 do not seem to have been relieved by his activities and associations at the art school. In later life his memories of Camberwell were, for the most part, negative. For instance, in an essay on the American art historian Bernard Berenson, he writes very slightingly of 'the situation forty years ago in the suburban art-school of my youth'. The conservative Berenson might have spurned the innovations of Post-Impressionism and the subsequent phases and emphases in the development of modern art but David remembers how worn out the traditional had become by the time he was a student. What he calls 'Academism' and

'Tradition' were already moribund and all that the student could do was to 'feel about, explore, consider the opposing opinions, of this or that teacher, attempt this or that in search of some criteria that might appear more or less valid . . .'[4] Years later he told a friend that at Camberwell 'a kind of faded academicism, the last dregs of the classical tradition were implanted in me'.[5]

Despite this lack of direction and sense of sterility in his Camberwell years David himself, and certainly many admirers and students of his paintings, have recognized the importance in his development as an artist of at least two of his teachers at Camberwell. The first was Reginald Savage, who introduced the young man to illustrations and draughtsmanship of a kind he had not encountered before. Savage was an engraver and in the mid-1891s had done pen drawings in Pre-Raphaelite style to illustrate Coleridge's *Rime of the Ancient Mariner*, a text which David was also to illustrate later in life. Savage got David to study the work of the Pre-Raphaelites, of Frederick Sandys and of Aubrey Beardsley, and clearly these artists also had an effect on his subsequent work as a painter. But undoubtedly the most important influence on him at Camberwell was the very lively and energetic part-time teacher Archibald Standish Hartrick, whom David would come to think of and refer to as a friend. Born in India in 1864, the son of an army captain, Hartrick was educated at Fettes College in Edinburgh and at Edinburgh University. He then went south and studied at the Slade School of Art under the-then professor, the Burgundian painter Alphonse Legros. In 1886 he moved to Paris to continue his art studies under Boulanger and Cormon. In the summer of that year he spent time in the village of Pont-Aven on the south-west coast of Britanny and he met Gauguin around whom the School of Pont-Aven was beginning to establish itself.

Returning to England to pursue his career as a painter Hartrick became a member of the recently founded New English Art club, a group which sought to challenge the dull conventionality of the Royal Academy. A leading figure in the NEAC was Britain's most considerable impressionist painter Walter Sickert. Around the time David Jones began at Camberwell Sickert was moving on to an interest in Post-Impressionism, and in 1911, in order to promote the theory and practice of this aesthetic, Sickert founded the Camden Town Group. Hartrick introduced the young David to Sickert and the conversations the young student had with this very established and progressive painter were to be crucial in the development of David's artistic career.

Hartrick was also a writer about art. In 1890 he joined the staff of the *Daily Graphic* newspaper and three years later accepted a position on the *Pall Mall Magazine*. In 1895 he began exhibiting his paintings at the Royal Academy. He was also, we can conclude from David's recorded memories of him, a very stimulating teacher; Hartrick's insights made a deep impression on the young David. Once, for instance, they had a conversation about the Wilton Diptych, the two late fourteenth-century panels of tempera on wood in the National Gallery, depicting three male saints presenting King Richard II to the infant Jesus, who is held by the Virgin Mary and surrounded by angels. Years later David recalled something that Hartrick had pointed out to him about the panels: 'The Wilton Diptych is thought, I'm told, to be French work, but has often seemed to me to be "English" in feeling, and as was pointed out to me by my old friend Mr. A. S. Hartrick the wings of the angels are gull's wings, or at least wings of wave-birds – this seems a very appropriate English "conceit", and an extremely interesting one.'[6]

In a letter of 1970 David remembers a visit to the British Museum with Hartrick. They examined carefully the so-called Battersea shield, a Celtic bronze of the La Teǹe period and David, the great enthusiast for things Celtic, was much pleased when Hartrick, on the evidence of the shield, concluded that the Celts 'knew what they were up to, Jones'.[7] David's final assessment of this teacher is to be found in a letter to Arthur Giardelli, a purchaser of his paintings and later a friend. David writes warmly: 'dear old Hartrick . . . he was not a great artist but a real one . . . at his best he could be pretty marvellous . . . I think it was being sent off to Paris in the middle of that Bonnard, Degas, Toulouse-Lautrec, Van Gogh era that made him just that much different from his English contemporaries.'[8]

The first name on that list of Hartrick's numerous acquaintances in the art world of Paris was to have a special significance for David Jones. For in introducing him to the work of Pierre Bonnard, Hartrick not only brought to David's attention an artist who would become one of his favourites, he also introduced a major influence into David's own practice as a painter. Bonnard's delicate and gentle domesticities, his sunlit landscapes and his habit of painting views from and within windows became very much part of David's art.

The work of the Post-Impressionists, which the young Camberwell student discussed with Hartrick and Sickert was also to inform his painting. This was a very lively time in the history of painting in London. The historic and highly controversial exhibition organized by Roger Fry and entitled 'Manet and the Post-Impressionists' opened in the winter of 1910–11 just a few months after David entered Camberwell Art School. Very likely he went to see it. But the principles of Post-Impressionism did not immediately become truly intelligible or useful to him. Only after his return from the First World War, in 1919, did these principles first encountered in his early years at Camberwell with Hartrick become meaningful to him – and then most powerfully so.

David was a small, frail boy in his Camberwell years, and well into his middle age he always looked a great deal younger than he was. He also had a tendency to hypochondria and was acutely sensitive to physical pain. One day, as he got down from a tram outside the School of Art, he was knocked down by a tram coming in the other direction. Recalling this occurrence in his autobiography, *A Painter's Pilgrimage Through Fifty Years*, A. S. Hartrick wrote that David 'was fished out from under a tram car one morning, fortunately uninjured'.[9] When the autobiography was published in 1939, some twenty-five years after the event David was provoked by his old teacher's light-hearted attitude. David wrote at the foot of the page in his copy of the book: 'This is inaccurate, for I had a rather nasty cut in the head and nearly lost the sight of one eye. – D. J.' Nevertheless his studies do not appear to have been seriously interrupted.

Later on in his time at Camberwell David endeavoured to develop his skills as a painter in oils, but felt he was unsuccessful and had to conclude that this was not to be his chief medium. One of his efforts in oil was a head and shoulders profile of a bearded and sou'westered fisherman. The tinned fish company Skipper's Sardines, had organized a painting competition to find a new label for their product. David's father, always keen for his son to be successful, urged him to enter. Unfortunately his very competent painting did not win a prize.

As the course at the art school neared its conclusion, David found himself in a state of great uncertainty about what he should do. He did not want to take a paying job as a commercial artist, but he had steadfastly refused to take the required examinations at Camberwell and so had no prospects of a diploma that would enable him to teach in the art school. Such wilfulness and intransigence may strike us as surprising in a person who usually seems so quiet and gentle, but, as we shall see, later in his career, he could also be combative and very stubborn.

By 1913 he was beginning to feel rather guilty towards his parents, who were continuing to support him and had paid his fees at Camberwell but could see no possibility of a diploma or a job that would justify the money they had spent. In the summer of that year David set off with a friend from the art school on a serious painting expedition, presumably hoping to produce some drawings and water-colours that would be saleable. The two friends travelled to David's beloved Wales. They went to the small farming town of Tregaron in south central Wales, and spent several weeks painting there. They had occasional trips to other places; they went by pony and trap to the remote village of Pontrhydfendigaid and then on to the ruins at the Cister-cian Abbey at Strata Florida. Dating from the twelfth century the Abbey was once a renowned centre of Welsh culture, and had a most impressive doorway with Celtic spiral motifs and a large number of surviving medieval tiles. David was greatly taken with this ancient place in the valley of the River Teifi with the lovely Cambrian Mountains as a background. The valley was gorgeously green and kites and falcons hovered in the bright, clean air.

It is highly likely that David painted at this place that so moved him, but no paintings have come to light. He did paint a view of the square-towered church at Tregaron in Impressionist style, and a lady who was a friend of his mother's bought this. But there is no evidence that he was able to sell any of the other paintings which he did on this visit to Wales. During the following twelve months he grew increasingly perplexed about what to do when his student days came to an end. Then, in the summer of 1914, the First World War broke out and his future was decided for him.

3

Soldiering
1915–18

DAVID JONES WOULD SEEM to have been caught up by the patriotic fervour that excited so many young men on the declaration of war in August 1914 – and his father encouraged him. Many years later, David found a letter from the private secretary of the Liberal cabinet minister David Lloyd George, responding to James Jones's enquiry as to how soon the government would make official the proposed formation of a London Welsh battalion. James Jones had stated that his son was anxious to enlist in such a battalion, otherwise he would have to enlist in some English regiment, which was not what he would prefer. David's father received a brief reply informing him that the War Office would shortly be authorizing the formation of such a unit as part of the Royal Welch Fusiliers. David was quick to try to enlist, but at his first attempt, when he tried to join the Artists' Rifles, the army rejected him. A small, slight, rather frail nineteen-year-old, he was told by the military doctors who examined him that he had 'insufficient chest expansion'.[1] He learned that a unit called 'The Welsh Horse' was being raised and having always wished to ride a horse he presented himself at the recruiting office in the Inns of Court. Here 'a particularly round man wearing an eye-glass' told him that since he had no experience of horses he would be better off in the infantry. Another rebuff. Undaunted he tried again and towards the end of the year, when the army relaxed its physical fitness standards a little, he was accepted. On 2 January 1915 he enlisted in the Royal Welch Fusiliers and became 22579 Jones, Private Walter David. He was posted to No. 6 Platoon, B Company, in the 15th Battalion of the London Welsh, as the Royal Welch Fusiliers were sometimes known. The commanding officer of David's battalion was Lieutenant Colonel R. C. Bell DSO, the Colonel Dell of *In Parenthesis*. Bell had recently returned from service in India; he was a stickler for accountability and once told David off for taking a barn door from an abandoned French farm to use as firewood. Nevertheless David always remembered him as a 'jolly nice bloke'.[2]

In the early weeks of 1915 David and his fellow volunteers did rifle drill in Hyde Park, and since no rifles were available they drilled with walking sticks instead. David's battalions in the 38th (Welsh) Division were then sent to the seaside resorts of North Wales for further training. David and his platoon drilled on the sea-front at Llandudno. They were issued with sub-standard rifles and wooden bullets and made dummy attacks on the hill known as the Little Orme just outside the town. Artillery units at Pwllheli with no guns whatsoever practised with telegraph poles mounted on the chassis of scrapped buses. Billeted two to a room in seaside boarding houses, and with training very easy-going, David and his new-found comrades found that those early months of the war put them into something of a holiday mood.

David's billet was a room in a boarding house shared with a middle-aged bandsman called Marx who played the big drum. He was a heavy drinker, came in very late at night and smoked cigars in bed. David worried about the place being set on fire. Sometimes, when Marx appeared to have fallen asleep, David would go and try to remove the cigar. But Marx, would always wake up and prevent him. Marx, the drummer, had a line that he repeated all the time, 'Gounod, Gounod – what a musician! And always drunk, thank God'.[3]

Then in August 1915 the Division was moved from Wales to proper training grounds at Winnal Down on the edge of Winchester and in sight of the tower and high pinnacles of the cathedral. Rifles were still in short supply and it wasn't until November, when the Division was informed of its imminent departure for France, that each man was fully equipped. They were then all rushed off to Salisbury Plain for a brief, intense firing course. On 29 November the Division was formally inspected by Queen Mary. This ceremony, to honour their impending embarkation for France, entailed the Queen being driven past the soldiers as they stood to attention in the pouring rain. Two days after this royal review the Division marched off through Winchester and through the rain-drenched Hampshire countryside and into Southampton.

In *In Parenthesis* David Jones described with characteristic vividness and fine detailing their entry into the port:

In the middle afternoon the outer parts of the town of embarkation were reached. They halted for a brief while; adjusted puttees, straightened caps, fastened undone buttons, tightened rifle-slings and attended each one to his own bedraggled and irregular condition. The band recommenced playing; and at the attention and in excellent step they passed through the suburbs, the town's centre, and so towards the docks. The people of that town did not acclaim them, nor stop about their business—for it was late in the second year.[4]

David and his companions embarked and sailed across the Channel in rough weather. They disembarked at Le Havre. And now, that near three years' experience of war that was to become the major reference point in David Jones's life, to inform many of his paintings and drawings, to figure in all his literary work and to be the subject of his masterpiece *In Parenthesis*, now it began. But the generosities and humaneness to be found in that book lay far in the future. Around this time in France, the patriotic David wrote two fiercely chauvinistic articles which were published in the parish magazine of St James', Brockley. They were entitled 'Is it worth it?' (to which the answer was a resounding 'Yes') and 'Somewhere on the Western Front', in which the Germans are described as 'the war-lords of Odin'.

From Le Havre his Division was sent in cattle-trucks on a journey north east across Normandy to Abbeville and thence to a billeting area some ten miles south of the city of St-Omer. Here the Division was formally amalgamated with XI Corps, under the command of Lieutenant General Haking, which held the Neuve-Chapelle section of the British frontline. On 5 December, the London Welsh battalion's third day in France, the men began a fortnight's training behind the lines, at the small village of Warne. On 19 December 1915 they were taken in motorbuses to Riez Bailleul from where they marched the remaining few miles to the trenches of the frontline.

The frontline was by no means a straight line and various 'protuberances' had been given jocular names such as the Maiden's Bulge and the Pope's Nose. David alluded to them in a piece of poetry he wrote much later about that Christmas near Neuve-Chapelle. He recalls the troops singing carols and reports his hearing about British soldiers greeting and fraternizing with the Germans in the spirit of Christmas:

> and speaking most factually
> and, as the fashion now requires, from observed data: On
> this night, when I was a young man in France, in Gallia
> Belgica, the forward ballista-teams of the Island of Britain
> green-garlanded their silent three-o-threes for this I saw
> and heard their cockney song salute the happy morning; and
> later, on this same morning certain of the footmen of Britain,
> walking in daylight, upright, through the lanes of the war-net
> to outside and beyond the rusted trip-belt, some with gifts,
> none with ported weapons, embraced him between his *fossa*
> and ours, exchanging tokens.
> And this I know,
> if only from immediate hearsay, for we had come on this
> mild morning (it was a Green Christmas) back into the rear,
> two to three thousand paces behind where his front *vallum*
> was called by us, the Maiden's Bulge, and ours, the Pontiff's
> Neb, between which parallels, these things, according to
> oral report reaching us in this forward reserve area, were done,
> BECAUSE OF THE CHILD[5].

For nearly a month over that Christmas period the London Welsh were taught the practicalities of trench life and trench warfare by an incumbent Guards Division which they were to replace. In the middle of January the Guards departed and the London Welsh assumed responsibility for the frontline at Neuve-Chapelle. During the next five months they were also moved about quite a bit within the frontline occupied by XI Corps. At one time they were at Fauquissart and far from the small town of Laventie, at another Cuinchy on the La Bassée Canal. A memory of this latter place lingered in David's mind and emerged in one of the notes to *In Parenthesis*, in which he recalled 'a nice dog I once saw and a French girl in a sand-bagged farm-building, off the La Bassée –Estaires Road'.

On 11 June 1916 the London Welsh were withdrawn from the front and ordered to march south towards the River Somme. They were halted close to St-Pol where for two days they had training sessions on a combat and assault course that replicated the German trench system on the Somme. Each successive wave pushed forward, carrying the offensive further, when its predecessor was presumed to have been routed or destroyed. These rehearsals were extremely strenuous and David and his companions were exhausted when they resumed their march south. It has been reported that the frail, small David was sometimes so weak that other soldiers had to carry the rifle of 'the poor little sod'.[6] After four days they arrived in Toutencourt on 30 June and here awaited further orders. On 5 July they were ordered into the area below Mametz Wood, taking over the frontline between what were called Bottom Wood and Caterpillar Wood. On 10 July the British assault on German-held Mametz Wood began.

At the beginning of the second day of what David remembered as a confused attack he was seriously wounded in the left leg: a bullet passed straight through it, fortunately without touching the fibula or tibia. Years later he recalled that 'it felt as if a great baulk of timber or a heavy bar of some sort had struck me sideways, in fact I thought a ponderous branch of one of the trees of the wood had been severed by shrapnel and fallen across my leg . . . the disproportion of the small nickel projectile and the great bludgeoning weight of the impact astonished me even at the time.'[7] In a dazed condition and intensely thirsty he crawled about in the midst of his comrades advancing through the wood. He dragged his rifle along until weakness compelled him to abandon it. Then he found himself looking into the face of a corporal whom he recognized as being from his own battalion. He had a kindly Welsh face and lifted the diminutive David on to his back and started to carry him to the rear. But a major, also a Welshman, ordered the corporal back: 'Drop the bugger here,' he ordered. 'Put Private Jones down immediately. Stretcher-bearers will find him within a short time.'[8] Stretcher-bearers did indeed arrive and transported him to Mametz village and from there he was taken by ambulance to the base hospital some miles to the rear of the frontline. He remembered it as a *'very, very, very* hot tent'. But David, who was to have many aristocratic women friends in future years, was much comforted by the sound of a nurse's voice – 'very English, very upper class'. He thought it 'the nicest sound in the world',[9] comparing it with the voice of his friend, Lady Clarissa Eden, the wife of the prime minister, Anthony Eden. After his wound had been dressed he was sent back to England to recuperate. On the little steamer bearing the name St David, on which he was taken back to England, he heard another voice, this time of 'a jolly nice fair-haired nurse with a strong Canadian accent'. She kissed the twenty-year-old David on his very boyish face and said 'You ought to be in a kindergarten . . . Twenty last fall! You can't kid me.'[10]

The next three months were spent in a military hospital in Shipston on Stour, a very pleasant little country town in south Warwickshire. Here he demonstrated – and not for the only time during his years in the army – his ability to get into trouble. The head of the hospital was a Scottish doctor, whose severe and bullying daughter served as the matron. One strict rule of the hospital was that the recuperating soldiers were not to have any kind of social relationship with the nurses. But David became attracted to one of them, who lived with her mother very close to the hospital. He visited their house and was spotted by the matron while eating strawberries and cream on their lawn. This disobedience brought him a severe reprimand.

In October 1916 he returned to France. It was a great pleasure for him to be met by his friend Leslie Poulter, who was a corporal in the Signals. Of the several important friendships that David enjoyed during the war that with Leslie was the closest. David once described him as 'not only courageously unaware but *extremely* amusing'. Leslie managed to produce some rum and some bottled cherries to help celebrate David's twenty-first birthday soon after his return to France.

Shortly after his birthday David was transferred to battalion headquarters. The intelligence officer there had learned that David was an artist and thought he might be used to draw maps and to go on patrol and make sketch drawings of the places where the Germans had set up new wire or other defences. Another of his tasks in the Field Survey Company was to assess the position of German artillery by judging the direction of their gun flashes. But he proved inefficient at this and was soon dismissed from headquarters and returned to his unit.

Meanwhile the unit had been moved to the north flank of the British frontline in the Boesinghe, north of the Ypres salient. It was at this time that he met a Catholic chaplain who lent him a book by St Francis de Sales, *An Introduction to The Devout*. This meeting and the book were important stages in David's gradual move towards abandoning the Anglicanism in which he had been so devoutly brought up in his parents' home and converting, a few years after the end of the war, to Roman Catholicism.

At about the same time, just after his return to duty, a rather strange experience also contributed to his religious development. This was his first sight of the celebrating of the Catholic Mass. Delicate and rather sickly, David felt the cold very badly at the front, and when he was in the rear of the trenches he would often go searching for wood with which to build himself a fire. One dark evening he came upon a rickety byre or outhouse. A light glimmered through a crack and David put his eye to it. Inside was a priest in vestments with two candles flickering on an improvised altar. Before the priest there were figures in khaki, some of whom David recognized as among the toughest in his battalion. David watched for a while but then moved on. Years later he recalled that 'I didn't think that I ought to stay long as it seemed rather like an uninitiated bloke prying on the Mysteries of a Cult. But it made a big impression on me'.[11]

Eleven months after David's return to duty, the battalion was moved to the south of Armentières to participate in the opening stages of the Passchendaele offensive. They were ordered to drive the Germans from a small but commanding hill called Pilkan Ridge. David later remembered the approach to it as 'a terrain of churned-up mud, water-brimming shell-craters, not a yard of "dead ground" not a fold of earth the length of y'r body and . . . heavy mortars operating from behind each stark ridge'.[12]

It was not long before David was withdrawn from this area of combat and posted to a reserve group. After a few days here he was sent to Battalion Nuclear Reserve, some distance behind the Front. The Reserve had a macabre function: a group of soldiers was kept in safety in order that they could give continuity to the battalion's identity in the event that all their comrades at the front were killed. When it was his turn to return to frontline duty, the battalion was transferred further south to a section of the line known as

Bois Grenier. It was a place that surprised the British soldiers by its quietness. Here war seemed to be in abeyance, there was hardly any combat at all. Occasionally the German artillery would start up, but otherwise nothing. David and his companions discovered that their predecessors in these trenches had even had time to grow convolvulus and other floral creeping plants on the side of the communication trench. He recalled that the place was sufficiently safe for a 'small French boy to come along the road blowing a little metal horn of some sort, with packages of French newspapers . . . for anyone who wanted to buy them'.[13]

They remained in this comparatively tranquil place from the autumn of 1917 until February 1918. Then David became seriously ill with trench fever, a most debilitating illness, transmitted by rats and other vermin, and highly infectious. He said that it felt 'like the worst imaginable type of flu', and was sent to a hospital behind the lines where he remained for several months.

Not long after his return to duty his battalion was withdrawn from France and sent to the west of Ireland. With the end of the war now in sight independence was becoming an urgent issue for Irish nationalists. The British prime minister Lloyd George and his government were not in a conciliatory mood regarding this matter. David's battalion was among several that were sent to Ireland to ensure the maintenance of the status quo.

The London Welsh soldiers were stationed at Limerick. During this period of David's army service there was another occasion on which he again showed the combative, stroppy side to his character. Years later he remembered 'very stupidly' crossing swords with a regimental sergeant major and as a result being put 'inside for three days, in a positively "medieval" dungeon in Ireland'. It was, he recalled 'an extremely unpleasant experience'.[14] The incident occurred after David had injured his ankle while going over an assault course. The medical officer treated his injury and supplied him with a stick to aid his walking. Subsequently encountering the regimental sergeant major, David was told by him to put down the stick. Three times David refused and, as a consequence the sergeant major summoned two soldiers and ordered them to fix bayonets and escort David to the guardroom where he would be charged. He was fortunate that the charge was reduced from 'refusing to obey an order' to 'hesitating to obey an order'. David later attributed the whole episode to the bad atmosphere among the NCOs at Limerick; they thought that the men who had fought in France needed smartening up in every way. For David, however, Limerick camp was simply a place of 'bull'.

It seems likely that it was this same sergeant major who was involved in another unpleasant experience for David during his time in Limerick. It is described in 'The Great Bell', a poem by the Irish poet John Montague, which reports conversations with David during the last five years of his life. David relates how he was in one of the battalions that were paraded with fixed bayonets through the streets of Limerick. The parade was an imperialistic act intended by the British authorities to caution the Irish. A poor old Irish woman in a shawl, wanting to cross the street, scurried across in the gap between the two marching battalions. The sergeant major knocked her aside and down with one heavy swipe and she lay crumpled up in the wet gutter as the soldiers marched past. The brutality and arrogance of this act appalled David. It is surely, as John Montague's poem indicates, one of the origins of his lifelong hostility to imperialism.

A much more creative experience in Munster and a

vividly remembered one was the sight of a beautiful young woman driving cattle. It was for him another sudden, powerfully impactful vision of the elemental feminine. David and a few of his soldier friends were passing a hovel of a farm where the squalor seemed 'not modern but prehistoric'. To David it brought to mind the era of the Welsh heroic tales collected in *The Mabinogion*. The floor of the farm was 'full of puddles and mounds' and there was an 'old hag making up a fire'. And then there appeared the beautiful girl herding cows: 'She was ragged and bare-limbed and wore a red skirt with a very wide hem of crimson velvet, and was a figure of great dignity, with flowing red hair. Moreover there was red evening sun. The whole scene was very like in colour-relationships to a painting by Mr. Graham Sutherland and perhaps something of the same feeling'.[15]

Shortly after the war ended in November 1918 David was sent by the army to Dublin, and voted there in the general election of that year. He later said that he voted in order to get off parade for a few hours; he would not vote again until 1945. In 1918 he presumably voted for David Lloyd George, the Welshman who was prime minister in the coalition government. In that hastily called 'khaki' election Lloyd George was hailed by the victorious coalitionists as 'the man who won the war'; he was much admired by both David and his father.

Finally, on 2 January 1919 in Dublin, David was released from the army – or more formally, given a 'certificate of transfer to reserve' on demobilization. On his return home to Brockley he considered going to Russia with Leslie Poulter to join the army of the White Russians and assist them in their resistance to Lenin's Communist government, formed just over a year before. But David's father quickly persuaded him not to. At this point in his life David was still uncertain of himself in many ways, particularly in religious matters and in his attitude to the Catholic Church. But his commitment to a career as an artist was never in doubt, and to further this career he returned to the study of art. Obtaining a scholarship made available to ex-servicemen by the government, he enrolled in 1919 at the Westminster School of Art.

4

The Westminster School of Art 1919–21

ON HIS RETURN TO civilian life early in 1919 David had a succession of formative aesthetic and spiritual experiences. In that year the National Gallery placed on public view El Greco's *Agony in the Garden*, which it had recently acquired. In the twenty-three-year-old ex-serviceman, just now starting the long process of coming to terms with all the many and various horrors which he had witnessed in the trenches, El Greco's powerful and dramatic image of suffering elicited, as he remembered, 'intense feeling'. And just a short walk from Vincent Square, where the Westminster School of Art was situated, on the top floors of the London County Council Westminster Technical Institute, there was another work of Christian art dealing with suffering, which greatly impressed him. This was the Stations of the Cross in the Roman Catholic Cathedral, a sequence of bas-reliefs by Eric Gill, which the sculptor had completed less than a year before, in March 1918. Still seeking to develop a style of his own, David was much taken by their blend of the Byzantine and the modern. He also admired Eric Gill's treatment of these powerful subjects and saw in them a 'cool restraint'.[1]

41

It seems to have been through some fellow students at the art school that David came into contact with Eric Gill's friend, patron and confessor Father John O'Connor, a great lover and connoisseur of art. The Catholic priest who was to play a most important part in David's religious evolution was a colourful figure. The model for Father Brown in the detective stories of his friend G. K. Chesterton, O'Connor was worldly, highly perceptive and eccentric. (For instance he would give his guests Marsala for breakfast and cigars immediately afterwards.) He may have looked the proto-typical Irish parish priest with his rubicund figure and cheerful round face, but he was also an intellectual and a serious theologian. In 1937 he would become a privy chamberlain to Pope Pius XI and thus acquired the title of 'Monsignor'. Greatly interested in the thoughts of Jacques Maritain, whom T. S. Eliot described as 'probably the most powerful force in contemporary French philosophy',[2] Father O'Connor was in the early 1920s the translator into English of Maritain's *Art et Scholastique* under the title *The Philosophy of Art*. David read this work and was much influenced by it. For him Maritain's argument about epi-phany in art was especially important. Maritain main-tained, in a way that is very reminiscent of James Joyce writing about the identical concept in *Stephen Hero*, that the true artist uses particular images and incidents to show the universal: 'Art . . . does not . . . stop at forms and colours . . . but it takes them as making known other things than themselves, that is to say as *signs*. And the thing signified may itself be a sign in turn, and the more the work of art is laden with significance . . . the vaster and the richer and the higher will be the possibility of joy and beauty.'[3] Father O'Connor's translation was an important early reference point in one aspect of David's multi-faceted career – that of the aesthetician – and O'Connor's conversation was a very helpful and stabilizing influence upon David during the religious and artistic uncertainties he experienced during his years at the Westminster School of Art.

The School, according to its principal, Walter Bayes, one of David's teachers, was intellectually lively, if under-funded. Compared to other London art schools such as the Slade, the Royal Academy and the Royal College of Art, the Westminster was, he maintained, 'the smallest, the least official, the least endowed'.[4] There was much heated discussion of aesthetics in the School at that time and the Post-Impressionist theories that David had encountered, some-what uncomprehendingly, before the war, now greatly appealed to him and some of his fellow students. He found that 'one of the more rewarding notions implicit in the post-Impressionist idea was that a work is a "thing" and not (necessarily) the impression of some other thing. For ex-ample, that it is the "abstract" quality in any painting (no matter how "realistic") that causes the painting to have "being", and which alone gives it the right to be claimed as an art-work . . .'[5]

David was not only interested in what was then, in England, avant-garde theory; though he was never an abstractionist, he also sought to bring avant-garde elements into his practice as an artist. A major drawing which he undertook at Westminster during his first year is a *Cruci-fixion*, now in the Tate Gallery archive. The dozen or so soldiers who stand around the three crosses are not Ro-mans but British soldiers from the First World War, wear-ing shorts and domed tin hats. As Jonathan Miles and Derek Shiel have pointed out in their excellent and com-prehensive account of David's art, *David Jones The Maker Unmade*, one of the soldiers has a pudding-basin haircut, such as was fashionable in 1919. David himself had such a cut and so did Stanley Spencer, who was at this same moment beginning to plan that great sequence of paintings of occasions in the war that would eventually find a home in the Sandham Memorial Chapel at Burghclere in Hampshire. A striking similarity in the careers of these two artists, who were later to meet and become friendly, is that, after their service in the war, both men devoted many years of their lives to creating a grand redemptive vision of that terrible war – Stanley Spencer in the Burghclere chapel paintings and David in the long-meditated *In Parenthesis*.

There are contemporary elements, too, in a later religious drawing from the Westminster years, the powerful and dramatic *Betrayal*. This triptych also portrays the soldiers who are coming to arrest Christ as modern soldiers; they are harshly linear figures, automata such as are found in the work of Wyndham Lewis and other painters in the Vorticist group. David's interest in the Vorticists, the group led by Ezra Pound and the painter/poet Wyndham Lewis, will have been encouraged by one of the teachers at Westminster, Bernard Meninsky, who had had his painting shown at Vorticist exhibitions. Meninsky, who before the war had studied at the Slade – and with the innovative stage designer Gordon Craig in Florence – was only four years older than David and the two got on well. In David's second year at the Westminster, Meninsky, still in his twenties, succeeded Walter Sickert as teacher of life-drawing at the School. David remembered these two progressive teachers, both very sympathetic to the avant-garde, with much gratitude and affection. In his final year at Westminster he saw a great deal of Sickert, and when he was asked, late in his life, whether the-then sixty-year-old and very famous painter was not very grand, David replied, 'Sickert! Grand! No, he was very friendly and accessible. He used to take us to the ABC and complain loudly that he had stacks of unsold effing pictures at home.' David always regarded Sickert, his teashop companion, as the 'best English painter since Turner'.[6]

One of Sickert's teaching policies was to encourage his students to work outdoors; at this time David did several pictures of the natural world and also set out on a walk through the Kent countryside from Orpington to Canterbury, sketching as he went. During his first year back at school his career advanced markedly when some of his pictures were accepted by a commercial gallery, the Goupil Gallery, for their annual salon. But David did not sell anything that year or at the salons of the following years: his prices were very high and some suggested that this was his way of hanging on to his work. All his life he was reluctant to part with it. In his final year at the Westminster School of Art David committed himself to doing a very ambitious oil painting. Based on one of his walking-tour sketches and entitled *Landscape in Kent* it was a large canvas measuring sixty-five by eighty-nine centimetres. The colours were dull but the painting had that quality of mystery that was to grow stronger in David's later landscapes. He submitted the painting for exhibition by the London Group in which Sickert was still an influential figure, but it was rejected, and a very disappointed David finally gave it away to a friend.

Throughout his years at the Westminster David worked hard and extremely dedicatedly at his art. On weekends and holidays when the School was closed he attended an 'old-fashioned atelier in Kensington near the Oval . . . one just walked in, gave a chap a bob or something, signed a register . . . tried to get hold of an easel or at least a stool and started to paint . . .' In this rather shabby studio in South London the 'model used to undress behind a torn bit of curtain hanging from a rectangular bent curtain rod . . . I really only went to get work done when it was not possible to go to the regulation place, I must say we were pretty single-minded, we just did drawings and paintings all day, except Sunday.'[7]

At home in Brockley, Sunday was, of course, very much the Lord's Day. But increasingly David distanced himself from the Evangelicalism of his lay reader father. At this time he often went as an observer to the Catholic sacrament of the Mass, frequently in Westminster Cathedral. He pondered deeply the words and the rituals of the sacrament and also the relationship between art and sacrament, a subject on which he would write a great deal in future years. It was perhaps to assist him with this latter issue that Father John O'Connor suggested that David go and talk to his friend Eric Gill, who as well as being a sculptor was a typographer, a letter-cutter, a wood engraver, an aesthetician and a convert to Catholicism. On a rainy day in January 1921 David set off for Ditchling Common, just south of Haywards Heath in Sussex, where Eric Gill headed a community of Catholic craftsmen and craftswomen.

The meeting that day was a crucial occasion in David's life: for the next twenty years his life would be conditioned socially, professionally, intellectually and emotionally by his relationship with Eric Gill and with Gill's family and friends.

5

Eric Gill and Ditchling Common 1921–4

AT THE TIME OF their first meeting Eric Gill was thirty-eight years old; that is to say thirteen years older than David Jones. He was not quite old enough to have been David's father but he certainly became a father figure to him. The son of a minister in the Countess of Huntingdon's Connection, a sect of Calvinist Methodists, Gill had begun his career working and studying in the office of the London architect W. D. Caröe. He also took classes in writing and illumination at the Central School of Arts and Crafts, the co-principal of which at that time was W. R. Lethaby, a highly gifted architect and designer and a devoted follower of William Morris. Eric Gill also studied lettering and before he was twenty had begun a career as a carver of stone lettering, chiefly for tombstones and plaques.

For nearly three years he lived in Hammersmith, close to numerous members of the Arts and Crafts movement who had many inspirational memories of William Morris, who had lived and died there nine years before Gill went to live in Hammersmith. Gill was greatly influenced by Morris's ideas, including, at this time, his socialism. In 1907 Gill decided, as so many Arts and Craftsmen had been in the habit of doing, to retreat to the country and he and his wife Mary set up house in the attractive little village of Ditchling in Sussex.

Two years later Gill extended his artistic activities by becoming a sculptor. He also became a Catholic and founded the Guild of SS Joseph and Dominic, an association of Catholic craftsmen or, as Gill himself put it, 'a religious fraternity for those who make things with their hands'. After some six years in the village of Ditchling, Gill, his wife, his three daughters and adopted son moved, in 1913, a little way to the north to a house they had bought on Ditchling Common. Nearby houses were taken by fellow artists and craftsmen whom they had known in London, and a community quickly formed itself around Gill. Especially close to him during this period was Hilary Pepler, a friend whom Gill had first met in his Hammersmith days. Pepler was a Quaker and a great idealist; he had been a social worker with the London County Council and had organized the first school meals service for London schoolchildren. He had great energy and charm and like Gill and other members of the Guild, he was closely connected with the Dominican order of monks by whom he had been instructed in, and received into, the Catholic faith. Gill and Pepler travelled to various Dominican priories around the country, often going to Hawkesyard Priory, the Dominican House of Studies near Rugeley in Staffordshire. (It was here, Fiona MacCarthy tells us in her biography of Gill, that he first put on a monk's habit, the wearing of which, he found, greatly added to the pleasure of his visits to the priory.)[1] Hilary Pepler was also a printer. He had bought an old Stanhope hand press and with it set up St Dominic's Press in an old stable in Ditchling village. He and Gill worked happily together producing the Guild's magazine, *The Game,* as well as organizing and financially managing the business of the Guild.

The year before David's first visit, St Dominic's Press was removed to one of the several workshops of the Guild grouped together on Folders Lane, a little way to the west of its intersection with Common Lane that runs north-south from Ditchling village to Haywards Heath. Guild members lived close to the complex of workshops; some had houses on Common Lane, others on nearby Fragbarrow Lane. All the houses, then as now, were screened by trees from the road. Eric Gill's substantial house was known as Hopkins Crank.

Eric Gill was a powerful personality: dogmatic, direct, argumentative and didactic. He was also a man of prodigious sexual appetites, which led him into numerous relationships with women in the Ditchling community, including his sisters and his daughters, Betty and Petra. But incest and promiscuity did not prevent him from putting the 'girdle of chastity' over the Dominican habit, which he had also started to wear in the Guild chapel, which had been created in a building on Ditchling Common. Nearby there was the Guild workshop in which Gill wore – without any underwear – the traditional workman's smock, similar to that worn by William Morris.

It was in the workshop that a rather timid and uncertain David Jones presented himself to Eric Gill on 29 January 1921. After they had talked for a while Eric Gill said, 'You don't have a very clear idea of the direction you're going in, do you?' David agreed that that was true. Robert Speaight in his *Life of Eric Gill* describes the enigmatic incident that then followed. Gill picked up a piece of paper and drew a roughly triangular shape with the corners not meeting. Then he drew a second in which they almost met but not quite. And finally he drew a third in which they met perfectly. Then, seeking to assess David's knowledge of geometry, Gill asked, 'Which of these do you think is a triangle?' The twenty-five-year-old art student replied that he did not know. Then added that he liked one of them better than the others. Eric Gill replied: 'It's not a question of being better; the other two aren't triangles at all.'[2]

Throughout their long friendship, now beginning, the two men would continue to have differing perceptions, but clearly at this first meeting David was much impressed by Gill and strongly drawn to him. He made up his mind that it would be better for him to be an apprentice to a master like Gill than to continue as a student in an art school. A little later that year he was acting as Gill's assistant by painting in the lettering incised by Gill on the War Memorial at New College, Oxford. By July 1921 he was staying on Ditchling Common for extended periods of time. From Desmond Chute, one of Gill's close associates in the Guild, David began to learn a new craft, that of wood engraving.

Desmond Chute had attended the Slade before meeting and falling under the spell of Eric Gill, from whom he learned stone carving. Desmond Chute was a descendant of the Victorian actor William Charles Macready, and there was a certain theatricality in his appearance and manner. He was tall, languid and very much the aesthete, swathed about with silk scarves. One acquaintance remarked that he looked very much like an Aubrey Beardsley figure. Desmond and David quickly became friends.

Wood engraving was not the only new activity embarked upon by David. Always mindful of the practical skills required in the making of art, Gill urged David to take lessons from the Guild carpenter George Maxwell, who had been a coachbuilder in Birmingham before coming to Ditchling. This would be an antidote, Gill urged, to David's several years of art-school training. Although David proved to be rather clumsy as a carpenter he discovered that he could carve wood successfully. This would later become one of his several forms of art. But he began, in 1922, by carving little toys, puppet heads, door latches and wooden spoons, a pair of which he presented as a gift to Eric Gill's daughter, Petra.

David lived in the Ditchling community, with occasional trips back to Brockley, for some three years. And in very harsh and uncomfortable living conditions. Along with other bachelors in the community, directionless young men like himself, who had attached themselves to Eric Gill, David lived in a tumbledown building that had once been a stable and carriage shed. The place was leaky and damp, the walls were only one brick thick and the brick floor sloped badly.

One of David's companions here, and one who was later to change the course of David's life, was Denis Tegetmeier, a former army officer who had been badly shell-shocked in the First World War. Like David he had a government grant enabling him to study art, in his case at the Central School of Arts and Crafts. With Gill he was developing his skills as a letterer, engraver and cartoonist.

To the married, more established members of the community, living in nearby houses on the Common, these eccentric but artistic young men were known as the Sorrowful Mysteries. David, however, was far from sorrowful and clearly thrived at Ditchling. One of the members of the community, Philip Hagreen, who was a woodcarver, remembers him at this time:

My main memory of David at Ditchling is of his utter goodness. He had an awful lot to put up with and he never blamed anyone or complained; the discomfort amounted almost to torment. He was lodged in a stable . . . Around and under it clay – the dregs of Noe's flood not yet drained off. David's mattress grew mildew and I don't know why he did not get rheumatic fever. Our workshop was a hut without lining or ceiling. The wind blew between the weatherboards and the floorboards. David pulled his belt tight to make his clothes hug him and kept on working. At that time he produced an astonishing quantity of engravings, drawings and carvings.[3]

Contact with Gill and other Guild members greatly aided David's artistic and intellectual development. Gill was a fine example of the dedicated craftsman, he was intellectually alive, always ready to talk about Fabianism, distributism, socialism and the social role of art. He was also passionate about his Catholicism and he undoubtedly had an influence on David's decision to convert. In a letter written in early March 1921, some six weeks after they first met, Gill urged him on:

> you describe your present state of uncertainty very lucidly. I hope you will soon find it possible to take the leap for in my opinion it is not necessary that a person should feel himself absolutely convinced on every point of faith.[4]

David's longstanding religious doubts were assuaged when in the autumn of 1921 he travelled to Bradford where on 7 September in St Cuthbert's, Father John O'Connor's church, he became a Catholic. This action made for trouble between David and his father. When he wrote to tell his father of his decision, he received an angry, reproachful reply. For James Jones, the evangelical, 'the Romish Church' had always been 'the enemy of progress and

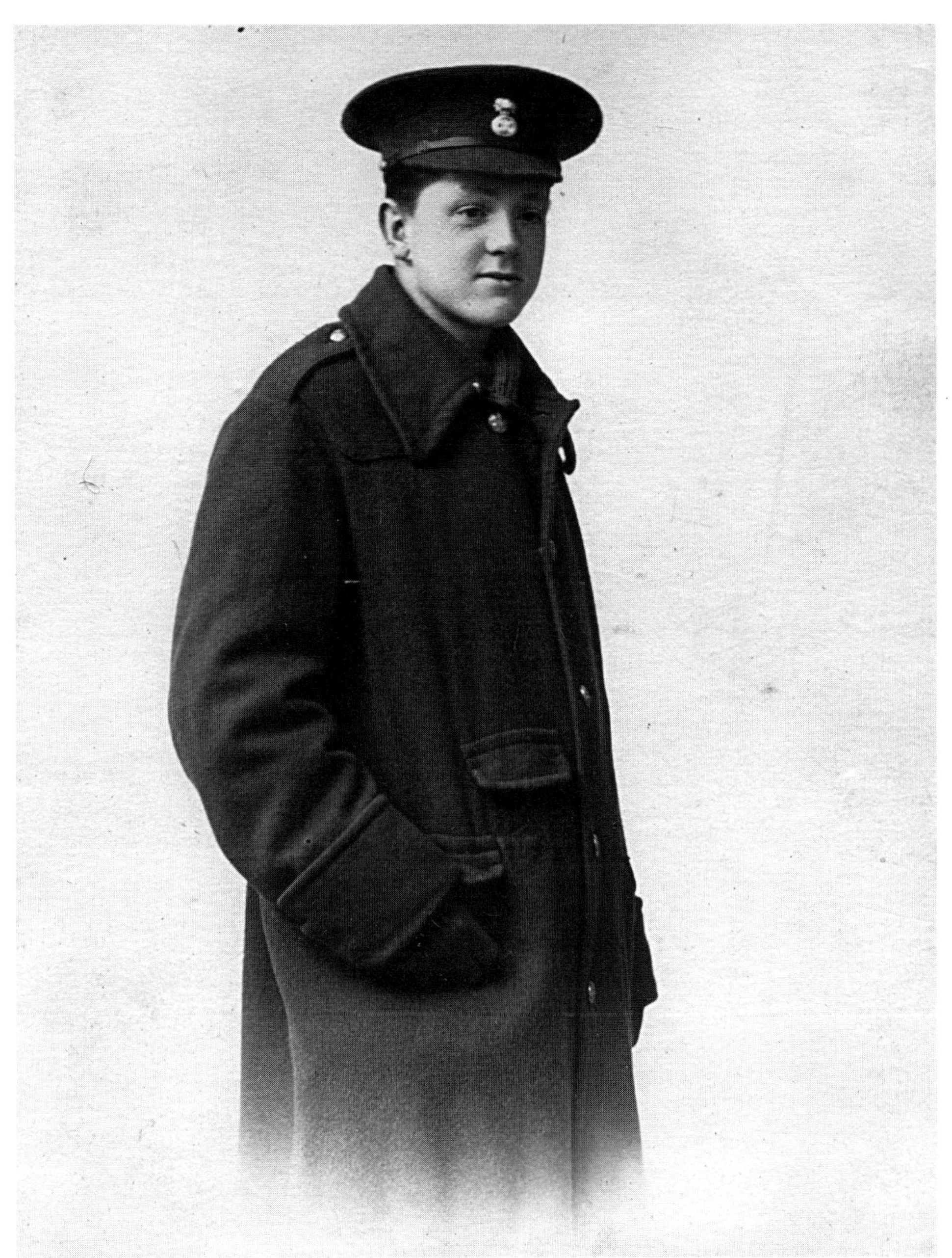

David Jones in his First World War army greatcoat

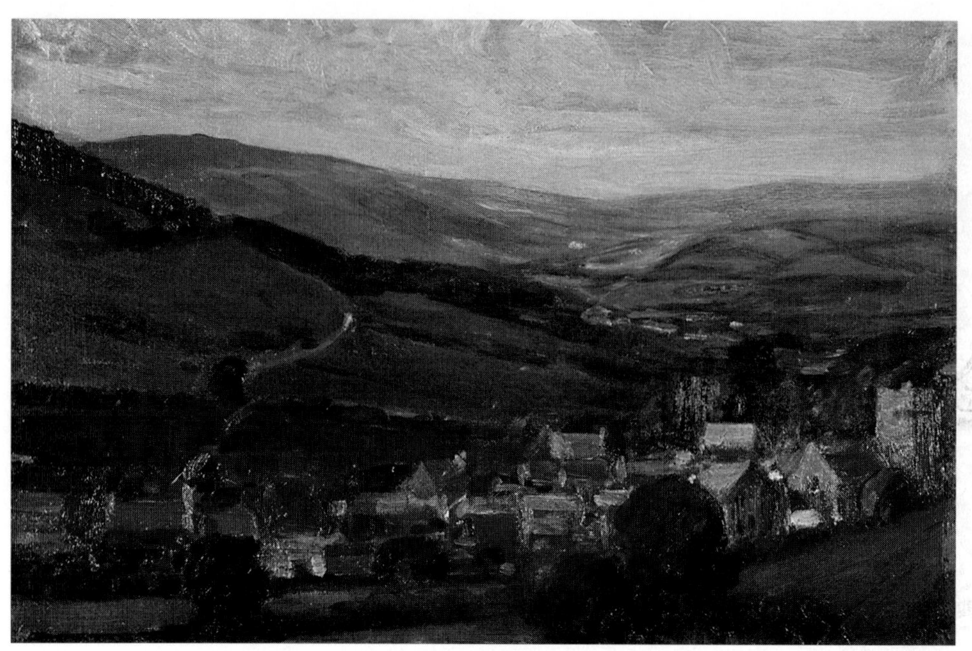

Tregaron

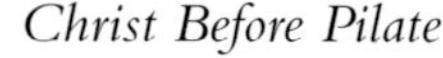

Christ Before Pilate

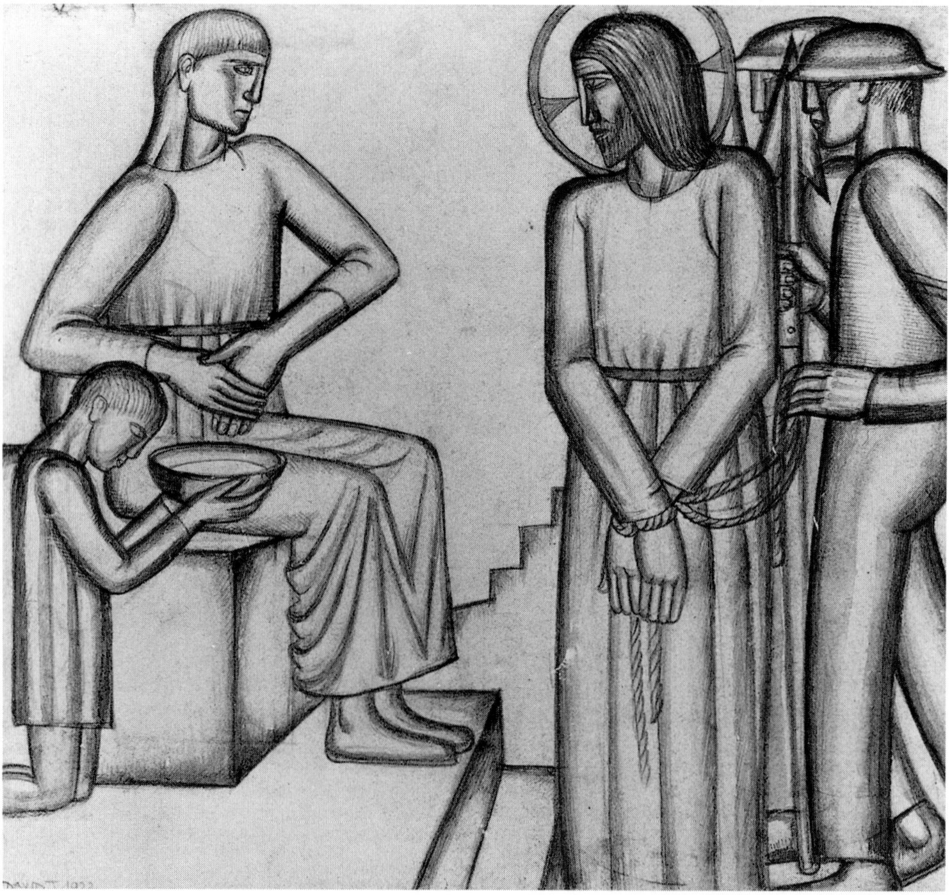

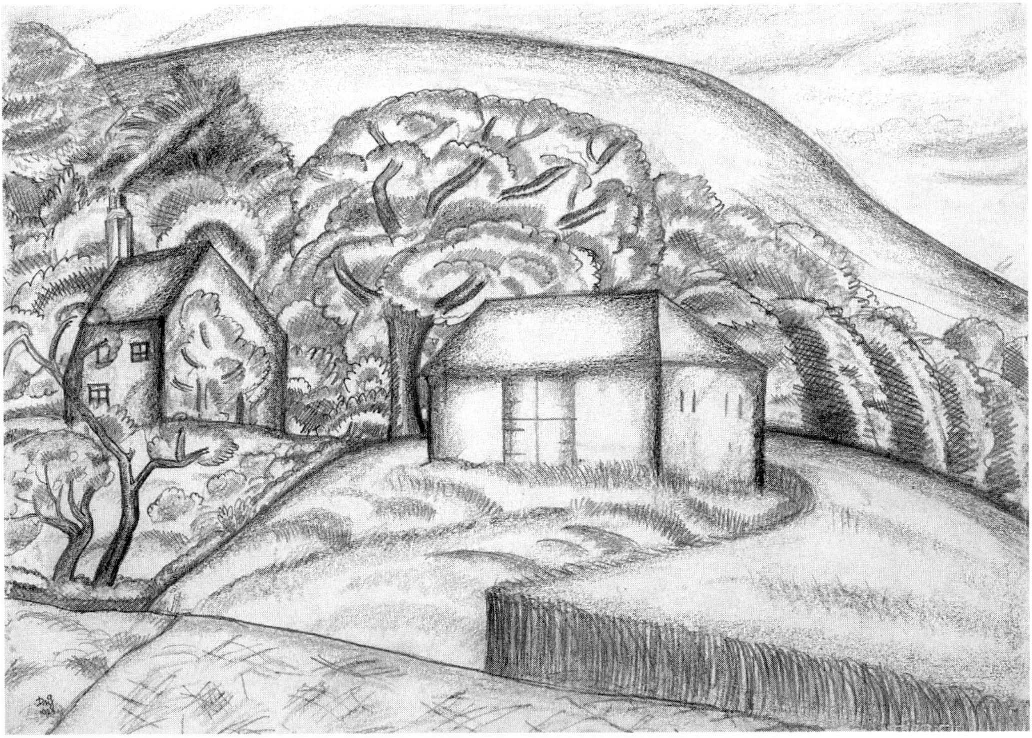

Ditchling Landscape

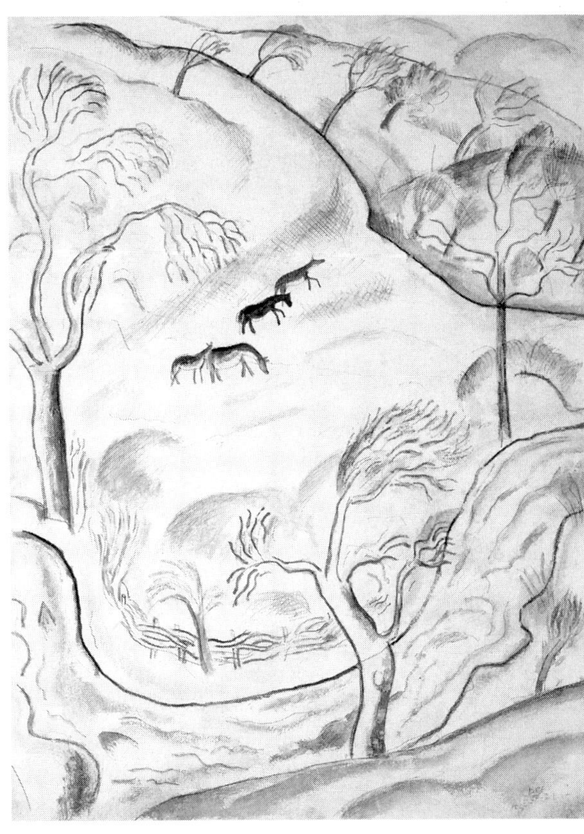

Nant-y-bwych (Horses)

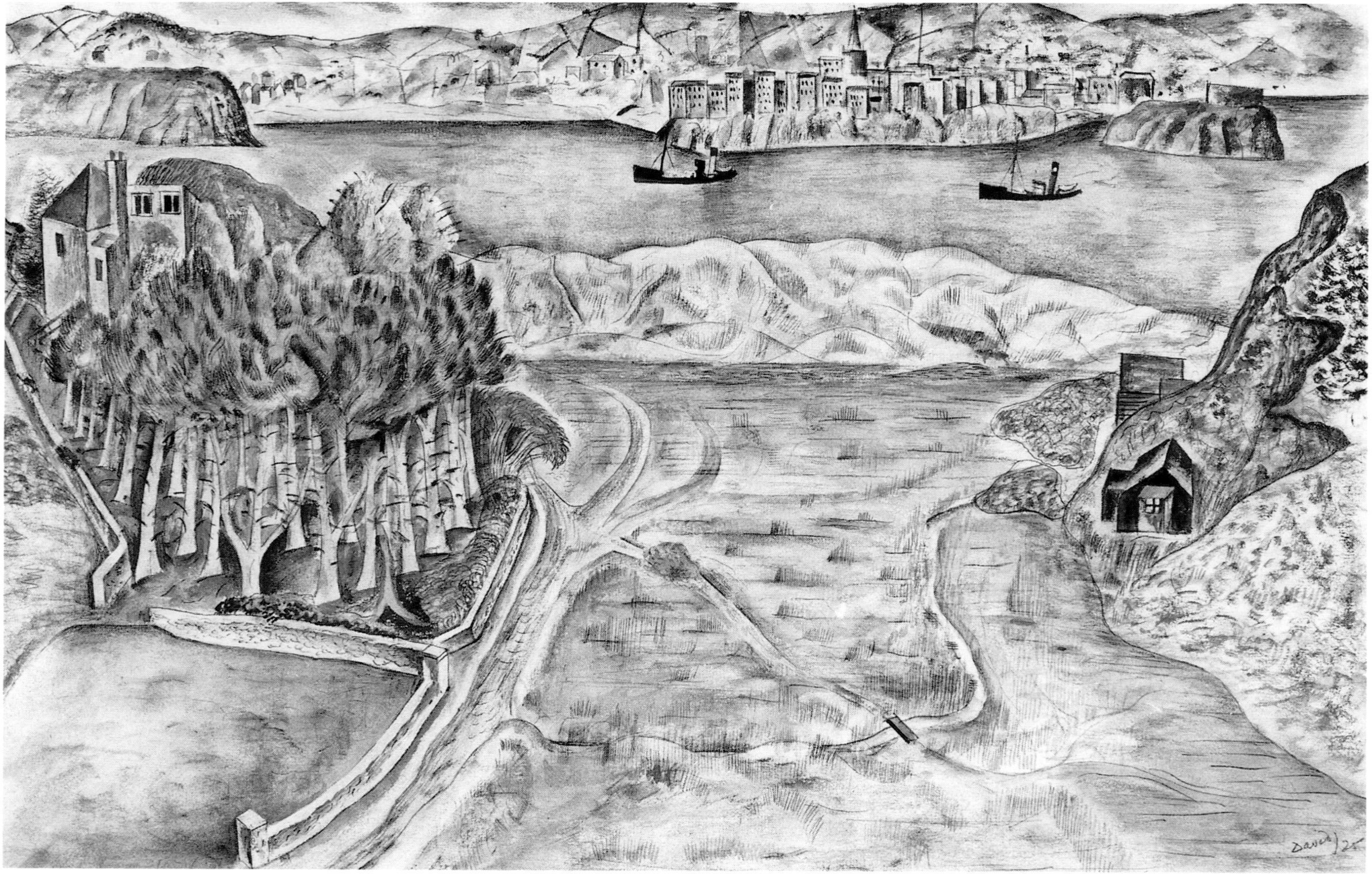

Tenby from Caldey Island

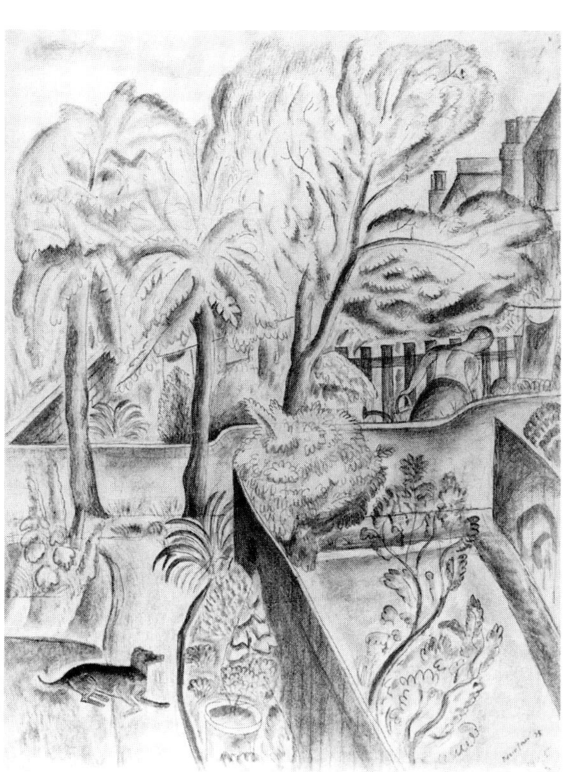

Brockley Gardens (Summer)

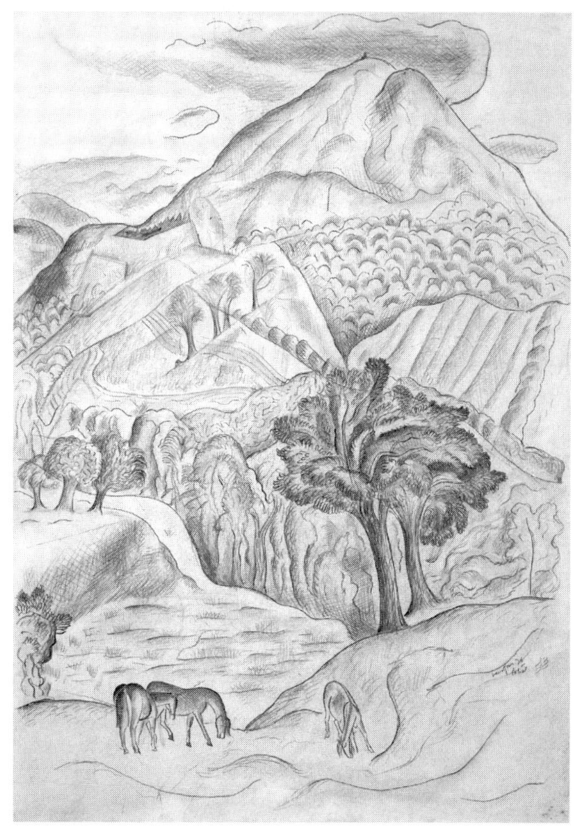

Y Twmpa, Nant Honddu

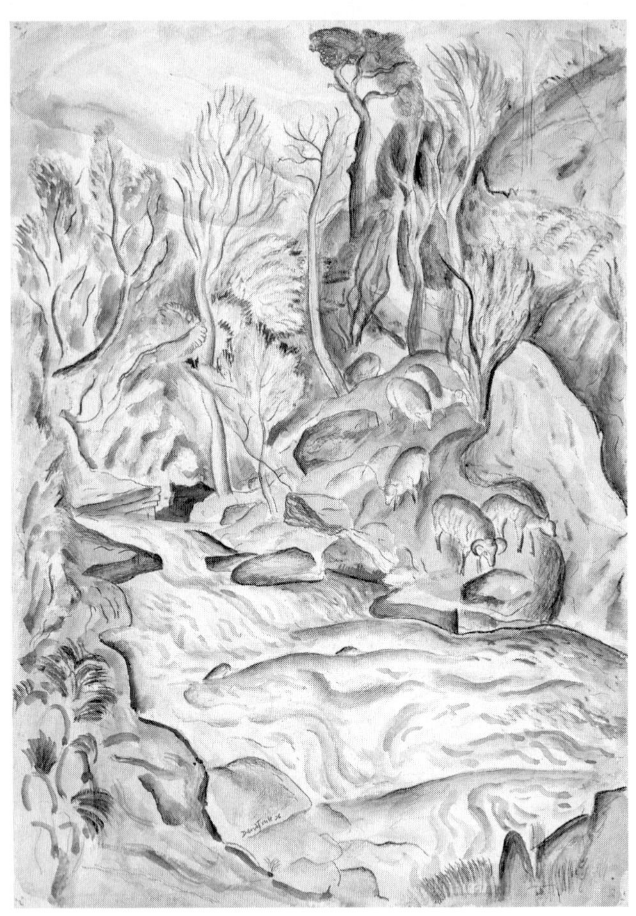

Pasture by the Water

Tramp Steamer with a Fishing Boat

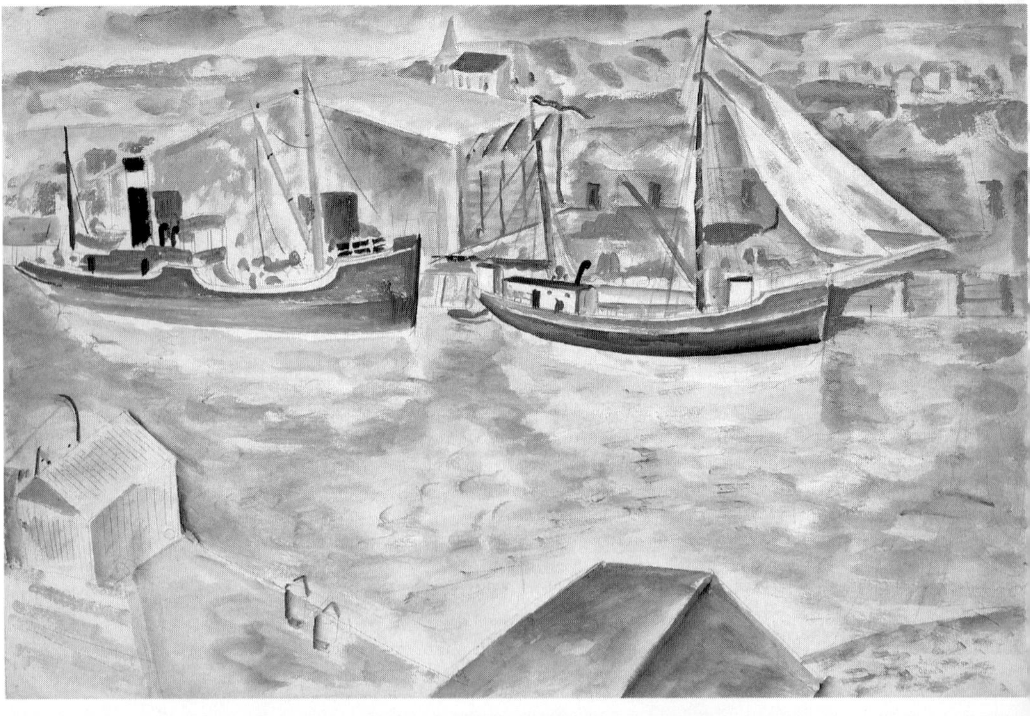

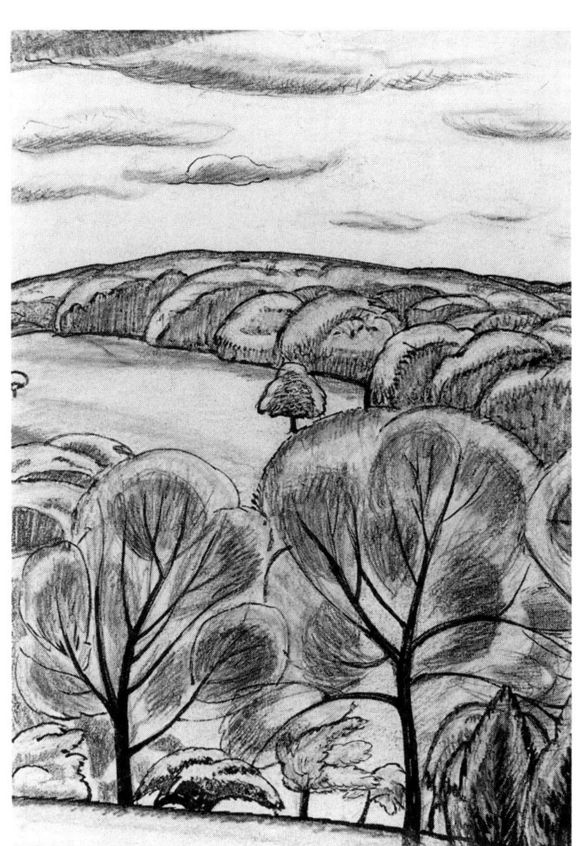

Wooded Landscape

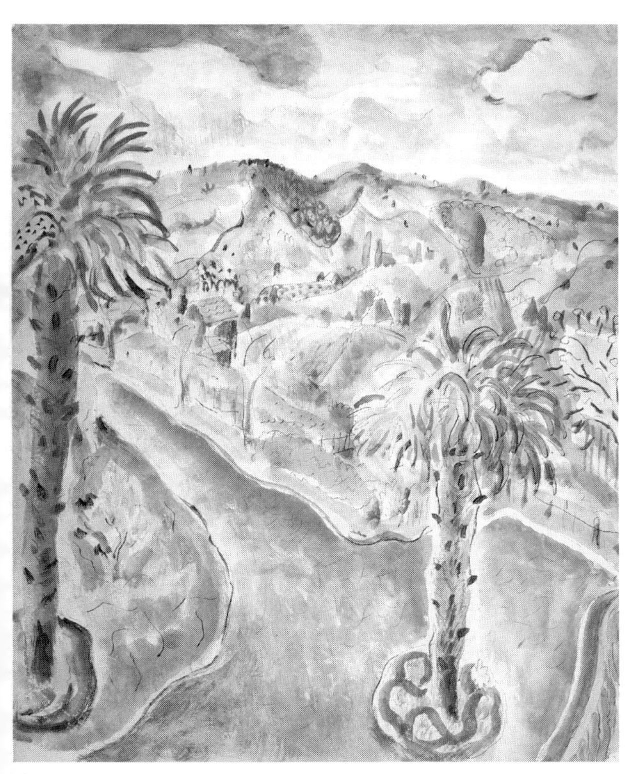

Two Palms, Salies de Béarn

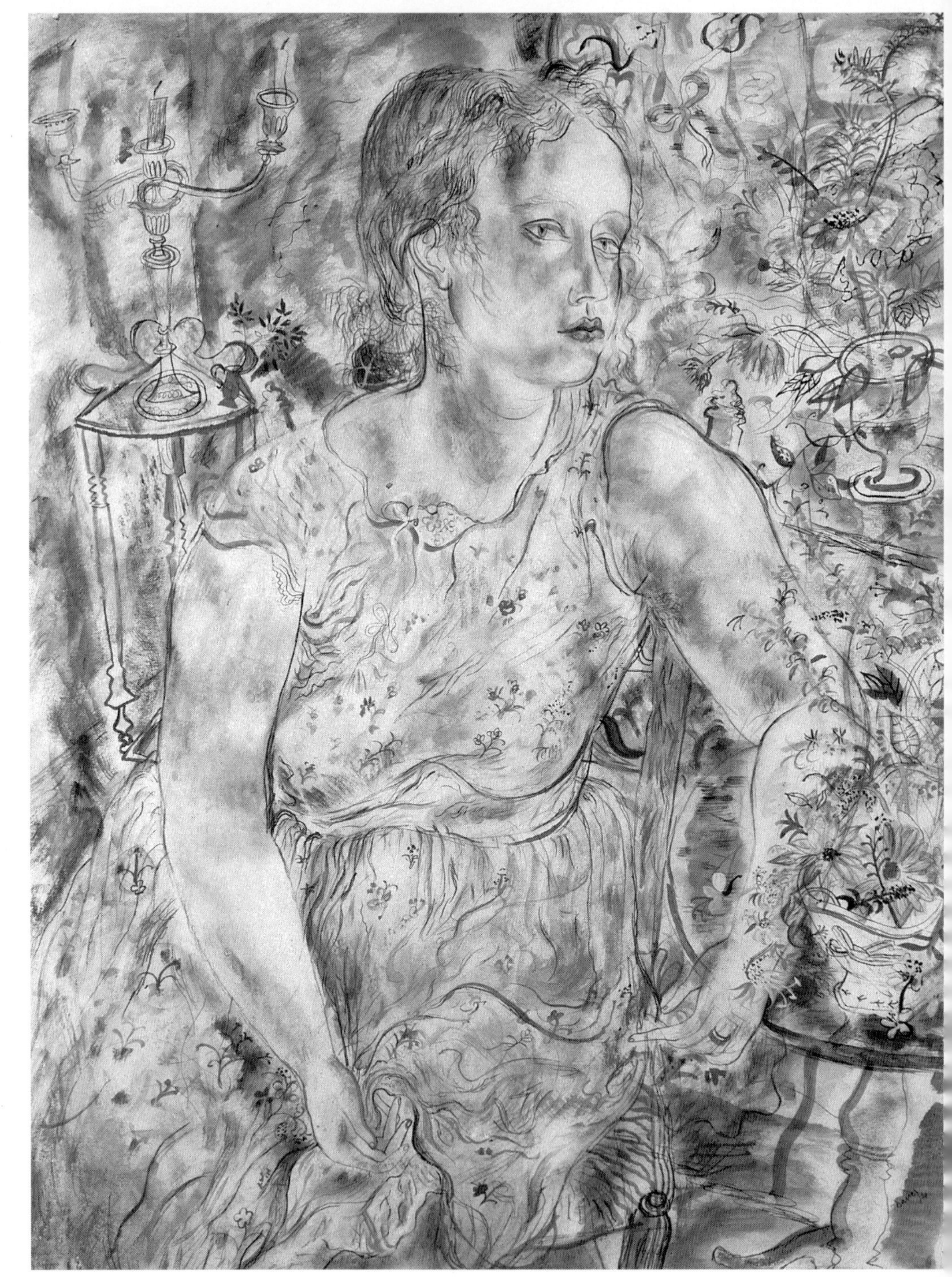

Petra im Rosenhag

enlightenment'. He now doubted his son's insight and common sense. Writing as a patriot James Jones also criticized his son, saying: 'By joining such a church you are limiting your loyalty, to your King, for his Highness the Pope claims first place.' He concluded: 'You became an idolator like the heathen in worshipping idols of wood, stone and brass . . .'[5]

At this time David was in fact producing the kind of religious artefacts which his father so deplored. In the year of his conversion he published his first engraving, entitled 'The Most Holy Rosary'. It appeared in the October issue of *The Game*. And in the following years he engraved and sculpted and painted a succession of works inspired by his newly defined faith, and in 1922 executed a notable drawing entitled *Christ Before Pilate*, with tubular, hieratic figures that show the influence of Eric Gill as well as that of the Vorticists. There are similar elements in an oil painting titled *Jesus Mocked*, which was done in the same year.

In 1923 David painted a large mural in the bleak room in which he slept in Ditchling Common. Its title was *Cum Floribus et Palmis* (with flowers and palms) or *Christ's Entry Into Jerusalem*. It is a primitive, powerful piece that still survives today, integrated into a private house. To honour the Guild's connection with the Dominicans David also painted a large image of St Dominic in the workshop which the Guild members shared. He also made a long wooden carving of the saint which he retained in his possession throughout his life. Not long after joining the Ditchling community he became a postulant in the Guild of St Joseph and Dominic which Eric Gill and Hilary Pepler had founded.

However, not all of David's work dealt with religious subjects. His engravings had come to the attention of

Harold Munro, the proprietor of the Poetry Bookshop (for many years an important literary gathering place in London) and Munro decided to commission him to illustrate a children's book, Eleanor Farjeon's *The Town Child's Alphabet,* which he was publishing. The twenty-six drawings are entertaining and amusing and their lightheartedness reveals a totally different side to David's mind and art from that expressed in the intensely religious pieces.

At the same time that he was developing and diversifying his work as an artist and especially as a religious artist David was also falling in love. By 1923 the face of Eric Gill's second daughter, Petra, recurs frequently in his art. Her face, with its very large, high forehead, and her broad fleshy neck are those of the Virgin Mary in a *Nativity With Ox and Ass*, a wood engraving done by David in 1923. That same year he made a carving of her head in boxwood, setting it upon an ebony base. The following year he painted a watercolour of her entitled *Petra Against Sheepfold*. Emphasizing the soft, full flesh of her arms and breasts, it reveals the artist's strong sensuous feeling for his sitter. At about the same time he also did a watercolour of the head and shoulders of Petra and her two sisters, all in profile. That of Petra looks rather hard in comparison to those of Elizabeth and Joanna.

David gave this work to Eric and his wife Mary as an Easter present. Close to the time of the Easter services and festivities of this year there was another ceremony in the chapel in Ditchling. On 24 April 1924, watched by the assembled Guild members, David and Petra were betrothed before Father John O'Connor, who subsequently wrote out the terms of the engagement. Petra was eighteen; David was twenty-eight. They do not appear to have shared a grand passion. Petra's uncle, Cecil Gill, observed that 'Petra in quiet and sweet acceptance of everything and everybody accepted David Jones' who was 'very devoted to her'.[6] David, indeed, regarded his betrothal to Petra as a vow. In a letter Eric Gill described how Petra sat and listened while David read Shakespeare's *Twelfth Night* to her, citing this as an example of their happiness with each other.

But that all was not entirely easy between them is suggested by the oil painting of his fiancée and himself, which David produced at this time. Entitled *The Garden Enclosed*, a phrase taken from 'The Song of Solomon', the painting, which is now in Tate Britain, shows the two lovers in a wooded place with outhouses which is very like a part of the one occupied by Guild members on Ditchling Common. The embrace of the two figures is awkward and wooden. The Petra figure seems to resist, even to push away her lover with her left hand. He, shown in half-face, looks boyish and desirous but also wary.

There is uneasiness, too, in David's face in a photograph of him taken with Eric Gill around the time of the engagement. The contrast between the prospective son-in-law and prospective father-in-law is considerable. Eric Gill, with moustache and luxuriant full beard, looks directly and very confidently into the camera, his hands relaxed, a cigarette between his fingers. David's hands in contrast are tense, his left hand held awkwardly and uncomfortably behind his left wrist. His deep eyes look through his spectacles in a way that seems both truculent and anxious. Gill's broad high forehead with its grizzled hairline contributes to his air of calm authority; David's pudding-basin haircut, with a sheen on it and no grey, reinforces his look of youthful insecurity.

The engagement was only four months old when the lives of Petra and David were dramatically disrupted. Eric Gill decided to break with the community on Ditchling Common and to remove himself and his family and adherents to a disused monastery at Capel-y-ffin in a remote valley just inside Wales in the Black Mountains. For some time Gill had been in dispute with his friend of many years, Hilary Pepler; they had quarrelled about the finances and the running of the Guild and after some unpleasant exchanges Gill decided that they could not be reconciled with each other. On 13 August 1924 Gill and his party set off for Wales. David watched them go. He had stayed on in order to complete his drawings for *The Town Child's Alphabet*, and in order to be with Petra who was remaining at Ditchling for a while so as to continue to learn weaving from Ethel Mairet, a community member who was a great expert in that craft. Later that year Petra rejoined her family at Capel-y-ffin, and in December David, after spending some time with his parents at Brockley, set off for Wales to re-enter Eric Gill's community and to continue what proved to be a problematical engagement to Eric's daughter and lover, Petra.

6

Wales and France
1924–8

ABOUT THREE-QUARTERS OF THE way along the main road going from Hereford to Abergavenny, a narrow and rising road to the right leads up to the ruins of twelfth-century Llanthony Priory. As you go up it, there is on your right what David called the rhythmic line of the hillside skyline. Sheep abound. Llanthony had figured in the arts long before Eric Gill appeared there in 1924, looking for a new home. Early in the nineteenth century Turner had painted there and it had also been home to the poet Walter Savage Landor from 1809 to 1814.

Some four miles further up the narrowing hillside road from Llanthony, just outside the hamlet of Capel-y-ffin, there is another religious foundation. This is the monastery founded in 1870 by an Anglican, Joseph Leycester Lyne, known as Father Ignatius. It was designed by a well-known nineteenth-century architect in a Victorian Gothic style. After the founder's death the monastery was eventually taken over by Roman Catholic monks based on Caldey Island across from Tenby on the Pembrokeshire coast of Wales.

Standing on a hill up to the left of the road as it climbs

northwards the monastery is a quadrangle of white buildings (which is now a private residence). At its south-east
corner stands the Chapel of Father Ignatius, which, a sign
today confirms, is 'A Dangerous Ruin'. To the north, at the
head of the drive, where you come up to the monastery
stands a white statue of the Virgin Mary. Nearby are two
fast-moving streams, the Nant-y-Bwch and the Nant Honddu near which Saint David, the patron saint of Wales, is
said to have had his cell. In a note in *The Anathemata*
David recalled that 'This stream is crystal clear and its
banks are ferny.'

It was to this remote place and to the long-disused and
derelict monastery that Eric Gill led his followers on a wet
day in the late summer of 1924 and at which David Jones
arrived on 22 December that year. Immediately he entered
into a new friendship. It was to be one of the most
important in his life and to endure until his death. René
Hague was nineteen years old and David twenty-nine when
they first met, at this Christmas time. René had been born in
London of Irish-Catholic parents and educated at the
Benedictine Ampleforth College, a boarding school in
Yorkshire. A brilliant classicist, he won a scholarship to
Oriel College, Oxford, but did not remain there for long.
He left to go to Marresa House in Roehampton to become a
Jesuit novice. However, this did not work out either and in
the summer of 1924 he went to Capel-y-ffin to stay with
one of the Caldey Island monks, Father John Woodford of
the Order of St Benedict, who was convalescing there. René
also taught Latin and Greek to a younger monk, Dom
Raphael Davies.

René was on a hillside gathering firewood when he saw
the Gills and their goats and other livestock arrive in their
rain-swept truck. He ran down to introduce himself and
quickly made friends with them. Soon he was very much

involved with the Gill community. A very big attraction for him was the Gill's youngest daughter, fourteen-year-old Joanna. In her memoir of René Hague, Barbara Wall summarizes him as 'classical scholar, ex-seminarian, wise, witty, drunk, holy, bawdy, very free in his vocabulary, and having a keen and loving interest in oneself, a very personal person'.[1] David Jones in his watercolour portrait of his friend now in the National Museum of Wales shows him as a sensitive young man with a long narrow face and sharp nose, long tousled hair and bright intelligent eyes looking through his large-lensed spectacles.

A shared exploit on Christmas Eve, two days after David's arrival at Capel-y-ffin, helped to cement the friendship between him and René. On that day in the evening the water supply to the monastery, which was a small tributary of the stream on the hillside, suddenly ceased. There was much consternation. René and David set off together in the dark to find out what had happened. They discovered that some way up the hill a malicious neighbour had blocked the little stream and diverted the water from the monastery. Clearly not everybody in the local area was pleased to have the Gill community as neighbours. The sandbags that had been used to damn the stream remained in David's memory; they reminded him of the sandbags that formed the trench parapets in the First World War. David and René hauled the bags away returning the small rivulet to its normal course and the water supply to the monastery was restored. As they returned home, the extremely erudite René was reminded of and quoted a line from the early Roman poet Quintus Ennius, which was later adapted by Virgil: '*Duo homines per acquam nobis restitverunt rem*' (Two men by means of water saved the situation for us). This also remained in David's memory and he adapted and used the line in *The Anathemata* in a passage speaking of

Christ as restorer and saviour. Some time after their return to the monastery David made a commemorative drawing of the two of them in their overcoats and spectacles, unblocking the waters.

That winter David worked hard painting watercolours of the landscape around the monastery. René Hague remembered him working out of doors in the bitter cold 'muffled against the cold in scarf and tightly lashed trench coat'. He painted views of Y Twmpa, the great dominating hill on the opposite side of the valley from the monastery. He also made his first copper engravings, including one of the valley stream Nant Honddu. One of his major achievements at this time was a series of watercolours offering different perspectives on the other stream, the Nant-y-Bwch. These paintings are full of animation, movement and sometimes agitation. As Merlin James observes there is in these works 'a dynamism and energy that marks Jones finding his form'. Illuminatingly, James relates Jones's 'growth towards a personal expressionism' to that of another artist who was important to David, Vincent Van Gogh.[2] Like Turner before him, whom he also much admired, David often enlarged the features of a landscape. As Jonathan Miles has remarked in his insightly account of these paintings, he 'dramatizes the already formidable landscape just as he sometimes exoticizes the vegetation'.[3]

David himself believed, as do commentators on his work, that he really found himself as a painter at Capel-y-ffin. The tabernacle that he painted early on for the chapel altar at Capel may show the continuing influence of Eric Gill, but the landscapes that followed are distinctively David Jones. As he himself observed, 'It was in the Black Mountains that I made some drawings that appear, in retrospect, to have marked a new beginning. My subsequent work can, I think, be truthfully said to hinge on that period. All my exhibited work dates from after that period, none, or virtually none, from before it.'[4] So convinced was he of his self-discovery as an artist, and so dismayed and embarrassed by his earlier paintings, that on a trip back to Brockley this year he destroyed most of them.

This progression in his art was not achieved in easy circumstances. Living conditions at Capel-y-ffin were as primitive and harsh as those on Ditchling Common. And the difficulties were compounded by the remoteness of the place. One of the monks staying nearby had an old Daimler but members of the Gill community had to travel great distances either on foot or on ponies. Unfortunately David's horsemanship was not of the best. René Hague remembered a time when David took the community's milk float to Llanvihangel to meet Petra. But he found that he could not 'force the obstinate pony, Jessie, into a smart trot, even though he stood up like an ancient charioteer and urged her on with loud cries and sharp blows from the slack of the reins'.[5]

In February and March 1925 some of his recent work was shown in the Lefevre Gallery in London thanks to the good offices of Eric Gill. In that latter month he went to stay with the monks on Caldey Island, having been recommended to them by the two with whom René Hague lodged at Capel-y-ffin. This was the first of several trips to the Pembrokeshire island for David. On the first occasion he painted *Tenby from Caldey Island*, a picture in which the distance between the two places is much foreshortened. But what dominates this watercolour is not the town, or the sea, or the two ships sailing on it, but rather a plantation of trees on the island. In a letter David said that he found this small wood 'thrilling, very thrilling', adding, 'I have nearly been demented trying to capture its beauty even but vaguely.'[6] Mysterious woods would continue to be an important subject both in his painting and in his writing.

On Caldey Island David also worked on some thirty-seven wood engravings to illustrate an edition of *Gulliver's Travels*, which he had been commissioned to do by Robert Gibbings, the director of the Golden Cockerel Press. David had come to know Gibbings through Eric Gill, who often visited him at his home at Waltham St Lawrence near Twyford in Berkshire. Gill practised fellatio with him there and enjoyed three in a bed sex with him and his wife Moira.

The Prior on Caldey Island permitted David to do his engraving in the Monks' Scriptorium. One of the illustrations, entitled *Ship and Long-Boat in the Bay of Brobding-nag*, is a representation of the hilly and indented coastline of Caldey Island.

Robert Gibbings was greatly pleased with David's work and immediately commissioned him again, this time to do thirteen wood blocks for an edition of the *Book of Jonah*. Around this time David was elected to the Society of Engravers, which had been founded by Philip Hagreen, one of the Ditchling Guild members in 1920. Other members were: Lucien Pisarro, Robert Gibbings, Eric Gill, John Nash, Gordon Craig and Gwen Raverat.

After his first visit to Caldey Island David spent some time at his family home at Brockley, where he did what was the first of what was to prove to be a series of paintings of his parents' garden and sitting room. During this period he was in the habit of shuttling backwards and forwards between Capel-y-ffin and his suburban London home, from where he now started to make excursions to Regent's Park Zoo in order to make drawings of the animals there.

Around the end of 1926 he made a return visit to Caldey Island and it was here that he received a devastating message. Petra had decided to end their engagement. Philip

Hagreen recalled that 'David suffered most grievously . . . He had taken the solemn betrothal as a vow. A German bullet had gone through his leg but the news that came to him on Caldey went through his heart.'[7] The catalyst for Petra's decision seems to have been the 'very fervent advances' that Denis Tegetmeier was making towards her, but there is also much evidence to suggest that her relationship with David was beset with problems. Photographs of the Gill community, such as those reproduced in Fiona Mac-Carthy's biography of Eric Gill, show a very youthful Petra and a boyish David both looking glum and dispirited. After two and a half years of being engaged and now into her twenties Petra saw no prospect of a marriage. Philip Hagreen recalled that David could become irritated by the lack of comprehension and education in his fiancée, who was ten years his junior. He was unable to commit himself. In part this may have been that he felt unable to support a wife on his meagre earnings and also because of his primary commitment to his art.

David was a sensuous man with words and line and colour and all his life he was extremely responsive to women, but his sexuality seems to have been frail, and for Petra, in comparison with that of Denis Tegetmeier, unreliable. After the engagement was broken off, Eric Gill commented to Desmond Chute: 'Poor old DJ was v. cut up at first but he's alright now and really much happier I think. The idea of marriage "put the wind up him" horribly – it was an impending doom – and fond as he was of Petra it was not "married love".'[8] In later life, when reviewing his sexual experiences, David told his doctors that he and Petra had engaged in mutual masturbation. But clearly this did not help to further the relationship. One onlooker, David's new friend H. S. (Jim) Ede, a curator at the Tate Gallery, thought that David was too deferential to Petra, insufficiently assertive in his efforts to husband her. Perhaps this is what a friend of the Gills was referring to when he re-marked that Petra 'would have devoured Jones'.[9] At the time, Jim Ede wrote to David: 'You need, I am sure, physical expression of your mental attitude . . . You are ill for Petra and the blank it has made. If you *know* it is Petra and not the blank, can't you go for her and *insist*. It is nonsense that she knows better than you.'[10] But David accepted Petra's unilateral decision and did not insist.

Petra went on to marry Denis Tegetmeier. The wedding took place in January 1930 in the Roman Catholic church of St Augustine's in High Wycombe in Buckinghamshire. The two witnesses whose names appear on the marriage certificate of Petra and Denis are Eric Gill and David Michael Jones. Over time it seems that Petra and David developed a relationship based on friendship and he painted several fine portraits of her. An especially fine one is *Petra im Rosenhag*, which shows her pregnant, with bare, soft arms, full lips, a sultry gaze and her flowered skirt pulled up provocatively. Prominent on her left hand is the gold wedding ring given to her by Denis Tegetmeier.

In the aftermath of the break with Petra David did not return to Capel-y-ffin but his friendship with Eric Gill con-tinued unabated. In April 1927, some months after Petra had informed him of her decision he and Gill held a joint exhibi-tion at the St George's Gallery, just off Hanover Square, in London. Gill, who was not primarily an easel artist, exhibited some rather simple drawings and David showed twenty-seven watercolours done at Capel, Caldey Island and Brock-ley. Those painted at Brockley included *The Suburban Order* and *The Dog on the Sofa*, affectionate, compassionate images of his parents' lower middle-class environment. The prices that David asked for his paintings were far higher than those asked by Eric Gill for his.

David's emergence into the art world and the art market of the day was significantly furthered when, a little later on in 1927, he came to know another friend of Eric Gill, Douglas Cleverdon, a Bristol bookseller who also dealt in etchings, engravings and modern fine printing. Cleverdon had a flat and a studio above his shop in Bristol and David stayed with him and his wife that summer. Here they worked on plans for David to do copper engravings for an edition of Coleridge's *Rime of the Ancient Mariner*, which Cleverdon wished to bring out. David also did watercolours of Bristol and visited its zoo to draw the animals.

The edition of Coleridge's poem was to have eight illustrations and a headpiece and a tailpiece. The poem was important to David throughout his life, figuring in both his writing and his art. Towards the end of his life he wrote a major essay on the poem and on his experience of making the engravings for it. At first he was very aware of his lack of expertise in the medium of copper engraving, and decided that 'nothing elaborate should be attempted'.[11] Nevertheless the sequence is very impressive and contains some highly dramatic images. The dizzying depiction of the shooting of the albatross is especially memorable.

In January of the following year, 1928, David's work and achievements gained further recognition when he was elected to the 7 and 5 Society, after being proposed by Ben Nicholson. This exhibiting society, originally comprising seven painters and five sculptors, was founded in 1920 and was one of the most progressive and vital of its kind in London. In 1926 Ben Nicholson, who became Britain's leading abstract painter was elected to be its chairman. David's admission signified that he had truly arrived at the centre of artistic life of the country. In the 7 and 5 exhibition of 1928 David showed an oil painting based on one of the Regent's Park animal sketches. It is a striking piece entitled *Elephant*; the animal is given a pinkish hue in a Matisse-like distortion of colour.

In April 1928 David accompanied the Gills and Eric's secretary-cum-live-in lover, Elizabeth Bill, on a trip to France – it was David's first time in France since his return from the war. They went to Salies-de-Béarn in the Basque country of south-western France where Elizabeth Bill had a villa. They travelled via Chartres and here David and Eric had an intense argument about the different achievements represented by Chartres cathedral and the church of St Pierre. David preferred the austere church to the great twelfth century cathedral with its famous carvings and stained glass. The two men continued their exchanges in their overnight train to Toulouse, keeping the other passengers awake.

Soon after their arrival the Gills took David on a thorough tour of Salies-de-Béarn. The little town and its surrounding landscape was subsequently to have a profound effect on David's style of painting. Situated in the foothills of the road from Pau to Bayonne, as you enter the town from the east the first impression is one of immense charm. You go over a humped old stone bridge, le Pont de la Lune, beneath which the small River Saleys flows noisily. In both directions it is overhung by houses dating from the seventeenth and eighteenth centuries. The town is full of narrow alleys, lined with bright flowers. The Romanesque parish church of St Vincent, dating back to the eleventh century, has an imposing stone tower topped by a hipped roof of sun-darkened orange tiles. It was once a watchtower and an important part of the town's system of fortifications. David and Eric went to Mass in this church every morning of their stay. And, together with their companions, they often had their meals outdoors at the Café Central in the main square.

Eric Gill was a very enthusiastic guide to Salies; he thought that the place had 'a quality of goodness and quietness and even "holiness" such as could no longer be found anywhere in England'. He called Salies 'that heavenly Jerusalem in which men unite to praise God and love one another'.[12]

Elizabeth Bill's property, the Villa des Palmiers, stood near the top of a steep hill behind the parish church. Here the party was joined by Mr Anstead, a former lover of Elizabeth Bill, and the father of her child (he was later to marry her). But in the meantime there was a good deal of friction between him and Eric Gill as rival lovers of Elizabeth. Finally they were no longer on speaking terms.

David kept himself away from all the jealousies and animosities and spent a good deal of his time on the first-floor balcony of the villa where he painted a large number of landscapes of the Béarn countryside stretching away in front of him. As Nicolete Gray has observed, these paintings show a marked development in his practice as an artist. Colour became much more prominent than it had been before: 'now brilliance of colour had gradually been incorporated into the "carpentry" of his work'.[13] There was also a strong sense of the bright sunshine of the south of France. David also found a literary interest in the surrounding landscape and was greatly moved when his hostess, Elizabeth Bill, pointed to a distant spot and told him, erroneously, that that was where the hero of the *Chanson de Roland*, one of David's favourite works, had met his death. A recollection of this exciting moment would find its way into *In Parenthesis*.

On 4 May Eric Gill and his wife, both now completely estranged from Mr Anstead and the future Mrs Anstead, returned to England. David left Salies-de-Béarn too and went to visit Philip Hagreen and his wife, who were at this time living nearby, just outside Lourdes. Their house was next door to a convent of Dominican nuns who, David reported in a letter, sang 'the office with a more marvellous beauty than I have before heard'.[14] He was moved to do a painting of them which he entitled *Dominican Lay Sisters in a Rose Garden*, a charming piece which shows the nuns picking roses against the two backgrounds of a white garden wall and the dramatic mountains beyond. Another fine and vibrant work done at Lourdes in pencil, water-colours and gouache is *Montes et Omnes Colles*, based on the landscape near the famous shrine and taking its title from Psalm 148, 'Praise ye the Lord . . . mountains, and all hills'.

David could represent the local landscape sacramentally but Lourdes as a place of pilgrimage appalled him as an intellectually and theologically fastidious Catholic. He hated the 'ghastly commercialism' around the shrine and said that visiting the place was 'like finding a Woolworth store on the summit of the Mount of Olives'.[15] Accompanied by the Hagreens, David moved on to Arcachon, a resort town on the Atlantic coast a few miles west of Bordeaux. He did a painting of the spacious bay there which later joined Douglas Cleverdon's collection of David Jones's paintings. David then travelled back to England. Settling in at his parents' house in Brockley once more he worked hard on his illustrations for *The Rime of the Ancient Mariner*. He also accepted a commission from Stanley Morison of the Monotype Corporation to produce seven copper engravings to illustrate a book entitled *Seven Fables of Aesop*.

Soon after his return David learned that Eric Gill was considering leaving Capel-y-ffin. Its remoteness was becoming too much for him. Denis Tegetmeier had discovered a complex of farm buildings and dwellings that was available at Pigotts Farm near High Wycombe in Buckinghamshire. He recommended it to Gill who finally decided to settle there with his family and followers. On 11 October 1928 the move to Pigotts was completed. The Capel-y-ffin chapter in Eric Gill's life and in that of David Jones was suddenly at an end. David was soon a regular visitor at Pigotts and in the coming years, in a life that became increasingly nomadic, Pigotts would be one of his several recurrent destinations.

Another regular port of call for him was Portslade, on the Sussex coast near Brighton. Here his parents had access to a summer holiday home, owned by his father's employer, right on the sea. In his autobiographical essay 'Illo Tempore' David remembered how the stone-built bungalow was built 'literally on the sea margin, so that if the weather were at all rough, surf and spray broke on the seaward balconies'. From a window in this bungalow David painted, over the next few years, an impressive sequence of marine views. A particularly memorable one is *Manawydan's Glass Door*: from a modern interior with window curtains that are violently wind-blown we look out onto a rough sea with an antique ship tossed about upon it. The subject is elemental: the forces of nature, seafaring and human history and artefacture. The title of the painting was taken from the *Mabinogion*, the collection of Welsh heroic tales that was another important literary work for the artist. The title refers to the door the Welsh warriors are warned not to open, lest they should see again all the terrible things they had experienced. The allusion would have had a special significance for David, as from his room he looked across the sea to the country in which he had served and suffered in the recent war. Some sentences from the *Mabinogion* concerning Manawydan's glass door supply the epigraph to In *Parenthesis* and thus connect the painting and the poem:

Evil betide me if I do not open the door to know if that is true which is said concerning it. So he opened the door . . . and when they had looked, they were conscious of all the evils they had ever sustained, and of all the friends and companions they had lost and of all the misery that had befallen them, as if all had happened in that very spot . . . and because of their perturbation they could not rest.

Portslade was also extremely important to him, as he later recalled, in that 'In 1928, at this bungalow in Portslade'[16] he 'began to write down some sentences'[17] which turned out to be the initial passages of *In Parenthesis*, published some ten years later.

So the year 1928 stands out as a very distinct turning-point in David's life. By this time, thanks to the many introductions made for him by Eric Gill, as well as his own talent and industry, he had established himself as a considerable figure in the English art world. And now he had set out upon that major undertaking that would establish him as a major figure in English literature.

7

Years of Attainment
1928–32

F OUR YEARS OF INTENSE and increasingly hectic creativity in both painting and writing that began in
1928 also started with the founding of some important new friendships. René Hague had by this time moved
to London and was working in a Catholic second-hand
bookshop in Red Lion Passage, Holborn. Through René
David came to know Harman Grisewood, who had been at
Ampleforth with René and then gone on to Worcester
College, Oxford, where he had won a history scholarship.
He was prominent in the Oxford University Dramatic
Society and played the lead in *King Lear* and in *Henry
IV Part One*. Harman Grisewood was born in 1906 and
was just over ten years younger than David. After Oxford
he joined the BBC, then still in its first studios on Savoy
Hill, off the Strand. His cousin Freddie Grisewood, later to
become a famous radio personality, also worked for the
BBC.

Harman Grisewood began his long and very successful
career with the Corporation by reading extracts from
Walter Scott on *Children's Hour*. Then, on the strength
of his beautiful voice, he became a radio actor with the BBC

Repertory Company, performing with distinguished actors such as John Gielgud, Peggy Ashcroft and Ralph Richardson. After acting on the stage for a while, he moved into administration, becoming, in the late 1930s, Assistant Director of Programme Planning. In the late 1940s and early 1950s he was planner of the old Third Programme, the predecessor of the present BBC Radio Three. In this position he was able to facilitate the broadcasting of some of David's writings. Harman Grisewood ended his career as Chief Assistant to the Director General of the BBC.

For David, a lifelong bachelor, for whom friendships were vitally important the relationship with Harman Grisewood was especially precious. It was literary as well as profoundly personal. In the Preface to *The Anathemata* a whole paragraph is devoted to thanking Harman Grisewood 'for his encouragement and for his critical assistance whenever it was sought, over the form here or the content there'. The gratitude expressed in the Preface to *In Parenthesis* is even greater. David writes: 'I do not think I should have continued, especially through the earlier stages, had it not been for the sensitive enthusiasm and understanding of Mr. Harman Grisewood.' Years later Harman Grisewood recalled the intense conversations about the developing *In Parenthesis* as they walked together on the seashore near David's parents' rented bungalow at Portslade.

Grisewood also recollected how around this same time, when he was twenty-six, he paid several visits to Brockley to pose for his portrait in David's small bedroom there. The full-face portrait did not develop to David's satisfaction and he became infuriated with it. 'Grisewood recalled that he had never heard such oaths before and eventually Jones took a knife to the canvas and tore it to pieces, amazing the sitter with his strength. The frail little artist had learnt from

Augustus John that to paint "you've got to be as strong as ten elephants," and so he became, when painting, vigorous and dynamic . . ."[1] The portrait in profile of Harman Grisewood that David finally completed exhibits something of this violence. The eyes, forehead, eyebrows and pointed protuberant nose are those of a sensitive, rather feminine-looking young man. But the hair, the sitter's jacket and much of the background are painted in rough non-representational, expressionistic strokes. It is not easy to be sure what this manner of painting says about the artist's attitude to his subject. Does the portrait suggest a serene unawareness in the sitter of the excitement he provokes in the painter? The title of the picture is surely intended as a compliment. *Portrait of a Maker*, alluding to *The Lament for the Makaris* by the Scots poet William Dunbar, who wrote in the early sixteenth century. Perhaps this was David's way of recognizing and welcoming Harman Grisewood's membership in the confraternity of artists and writers. In the course of his life Harman Grisewood published a number of books. He also contributed a great deal to David's literary career and reputation. In 1959 he assembled and edited an anthology of David's essays, publishing it under the title *Epoch and Artist*. In 1978, four years after David's death, clearly as an act of love, he assembled, edited and wrote an introduction to a volume of David's uncollected essays, *The Dying Gaul*. And in 1981, with much assistance from René Hague, he published *The Roman Quarry*, a collection of David's fugitive and unpublished poems.

The friendship with the London-based Harman Grisewood that began in 1928 deepened David's involvement with the intellectual life of the capital. During this period he got to know Jim Ede, whose numerous friends in the arts regularly gathered at the Edes' house in Elm Row in

Hampstead. In 1928, too, David gained another important friend who furthered this involvement still more. This was Tom Burns, who was the same age as Harman Grisewood. David was always at ease with, and stimulated by people younger than himself. At this time Tom Burns was working for the Catholic publishing house of Sheed and Ward. He later moved on to Longmans Green before helping to develop the Catholic publishing firm of Burns and Oates. Tom Burns lived with his brother Dr Charles Burns, a neurologist, in a house in St Leonard's Terrace in Chelsea. Their home became a gathering place for young Catholic intellectuals. It was in this publisher's home that David was to meet his own future publisher, T. S. Eliot. David became a regular at Sheffield Terrace and drew very close to Tom Burns. In 1993 Tom Burns published his autobiography *The Use of Memory*, the title being a phrase taken from T. S. Eliot's *Little Gidding*. In his book Tom Burns wrote a letter to David (who had died nearly twenty years before) as a literary device for conveying his memories of, and his affection for him. The letter began

> Soon after you began your constant visits to the house in Chelsea which I shared with my doctor brother, you became an anchor-man of our regular Sunday lunches and our not-infrequent parties. The first were serious and almost Socratic, often lasting late into the evening: the second were a rich mixture from the fringes of high bohemia. I can see you now, crouched on the corner of a divan with two or three graceful girls draped round you in earnest discussion. In a strange way you seemed to set the tone of the party. There was something magnetic about you; the small unkempt, unknown painter from Brockley – from outer space as far as most people in the room were concerned.

Trench language and the realism that lay behind it coloured your talk. It seemed to put you at ease with everyone, though there was no obvious common bond.[2]

But for all his new and exciting involvement with the literary and intellectual world of the metropolis, David regularly returned to the Gill circle at Pigotts in the depths of the wooded Buckinghamshire countryside. The settlement lay just off the road that runs from High Wycombe to Speen and Princes Risborough. The old brick farm buildings formed a quadrangle. There was the main farmhouse in which Eric Gill and his wife Mary lived and as on Ditchling Common and at Capel-y-ffin there had been created a chapel and various workshops. One of these came to be occupied by Denis Tegetmeier after his marriage to Petra Gill. Attached to this workshop was a tiny cottage in which visitors such as David could be accommodated. He was often there, sometimes for long periods. There was one especially memorable visit in March 1929 when he took Tom and Charles Burns up from London to Pigotts to meet Jacques Maritain, the French theologian, whose work was a major point of reference in the ongoing discussions in which these young Catholic intellectuals engaged.

That same March David underwent another significant emotional experience. He fell deeply in love with one of his fellow visitors to Pigotts. This was the beautiful Prudence Pelham, the youngest daughter of the sixth Earl of Chichester. She was the first of a succession of aristocratic ladies with whom David would associate in the coming years, but undoubtedly Prudence Pelham was the love of his life. She also cared deeply for him.

Prudence had come to Pigotts to study stone-carving with Eric Gill. They had first met when she and her mother had commissioned a memorial stone to commemorate her father and her elder brother, John Pelham, both of whom had died of pneumonia in quick succession two years earlier. The lettering on the stone was done by Eric Gill and his assistant Laurie Cribb. Prudence Pelham had begun learning to sculpt some time before in the studio of Antoine Bourdelle in Paris. She now resumed her studies with Eric Gill at Pigotts. When not staying with the Gills, she lived with her mother, Lady Chichester, on the family estate at Stanmer in Sussex, which is now part of the campus of the University of Sussex.

David found Prudence's mind 'heavenly', her sense of humour entertaining and her sensitivities highly acute. They quickly became very close. He did a watercolour portrait of her. She has a firm jaw-line and full lips and her luxuriant shoulder-length hair is pulled back from her brow. She has large thoughtful eyes and long arching eyebrows. These strong facial features and the broad, long, sensuous neck contrast with the fragility of the body and the long delicate fingers which David has modelled perfunctorily. This is all very different from the fleshy rendering of his subject of *Petra im Rosenhag*. David's new love has none of the rich physicality of his former one. Prudence Pelham's physical frailness was due to a slowly but inexorably developing illness known as disseminated sclerosis; only very rarely did she feel entirely well. She and David cared for each other intensely, but the relationship seems to have been less a sexual one and more a matter of shared sensibilities, ready emotional sympathy and shared interests, particularly literary ones. Often and at great length David discussed the shaping and actual writing of *In Parenthesis* with her as he slowly proceeded with the work in the years after he first met Prudence. It can be said that Prudence was the muse behind this great book.

At the time of their meeting David shared another exhibition with Eric Gill, this time at the Goupil Gallery which was owned by William Marchant who was also Gill's agent. David exhibited thirty-eight paintings, his largest show to date. It was probably at this exhibition that he came into contact with a buyer who went on to make a substantial collection of his paintings and also to become one of his most important patrons and supporters in the many periods in his life when he was in financial difficulties.

Helen Christian Sutherland was the daughter of Sir Thomas Sutherland who, from humble beginnings in Scotland, and starting as a clerk, had worked his way up through the hierarchy of the Pacific and Orient shipping company to become its managing director, and was extremely wealthy and the recipient of a knighthood. On Helen's birth certificate of 1881 he gives his occupation as 'Gentleman'. In the census of that same year his occupation is reported as ship-owner. At that time the family was living in a large house at 167 Cromwell Road in Kensington. Besides the baby Helen and her parents, the house accommodated, the same census tells us, a butler, a cook, two housemaids and a children's nurse. Helen's mother Alice Sutherland was also independently wealthy and left her daughter a fortune.

In February 1904, when she was twenty-two and now living with her family and their household at 7 Buckingham Gate Helen was married, in their parish church, St Margaret's, Westminster, to Richard Douglas Denman. On the marriage certificate his 'Rank or Profession' is given as: Gentleman. He had been educated at Balliol College, Oxford and had been the winner of the Chancellor's Prize Essay. He was five years older than Helen and soon to become the Liberal MP for Carlisle.

The marriage proved to be an extremely unhappy one. After the couple had been together for eight years, Helen filed a petition for an annulment of her marriage on 21 June 1912 in the Probate, Divorce and Admiralty Division of the High Court of Justice. The reason that she gave for her petition was that 'Richard Douglas Denman was at the time of the . . . ceremony of marriage and still is incapable of consummating the said marriage and such incapacity is incurable by art or skill and will so appear upon inspection'. The court duly appointed two doctors to undertake a physical inspection of Helen and her husband. The reports the doctors supplied led to Helen being granted her petition for an annulment and the final decree came through on 3 February 1913, almost nine years to the day after the wedding. On 4 February. 1913, the following sentence appeared in the Court Circular column of *The Times*: 'We are requested to state that Helen Christian Sutherland, only daughter of Sir Thomas Sutherland G.C.M.G., of Buckingham Gate and Coldharbour Wood, Rake, Sussex, whose marriage has been annulled, will resume her maiden name.' A year later Sir Richard Douglas Denman, as he later became, remarried and subsequently fathered two daughters and three sons.

Helen Sutherland now turned her attention to good causes and to helping individuals whom she considered deserving. She also became passionate about art and a great collector. Artists whose work she purchased included Mondrian, Picasso, Barbara Hepworth, Winifred Nicholson, Ben Nicholson, Christopher Wood, Courbet and Seurat, as well as David Jones. By 1930 her London address was Grosvenor House, Park Lane, but she spent most of her time, and kept the greater part of her collection at Rock Hall, a forbidding looking mansion she had leased in Northumberland. The place had a long history; one of the outhouses was part of a Norman chapel and there was a fifteenth-century Pele tower. The old Hall was reduced to a shell by a fire in 1752 and rebuilt fifty years later in the rather grim Regency style that we still see today. Here, some four miles from the North Sea coast and a few miles from the town of Alnwick, Helen Sutherland lived alone, tended by her servants.

In 1929 David accepted his first invitation to visit Rock Hall. He greatly enjoyed painting the views that he had looking down from his bedroom at the top of the house. One view was of the little village of Rock itself, with its stone cottages, lake, church and the recently built vicarage entirely funded by, and done to architectural designs approved by, Helen Sutherland, a very devout high Anglican, who gifted the vicarage to the Church.

Rock and its views proved to be a compelling new subject in this highly prolific period in David Jones's career. (He once estimated that during the four years from 1928 on he completed an average of fifty paintings each year.) There were to be many more visits to Rock. In fact just as much as Brockley or Pigotts, it became one of David's homes.

A routine was established for organizing his visits. Sensitive to his poverty Helen would send David the money for his third-class train fare to Rock. Then, somehow, David would find the extra money to travel first-class but at the last station prior to his destination he would transfer to third class so that Mills, Helen's morose chauffeur, who met him at the station in her Rolls-Royce, would not see and report his luxurious way of travelling. Although throughout his life David depended upon gifts of money from his friends for his financial survival, he could not give up certain luxuries, taxis for instance. When in London he always used taxis rather than public transport. He long retained a resentful memory of T. S. Eliot, much wealthier than he, who when they once had occasion to travel within London together, followed his usual practice and led them to an Underground station.

David concealed such expensive tastes from Helen Sutherland. He was rather afraid of this elegant but severe lady forty-eight years of age when they met to his thirty. She had a forceful personality and could be dictatorial; she expected her house-guests at Rock Hall to subordinate themselves to her lifestyle in every respect. She allowed no smoking or drinking before meals, and her guests were not permitted to be late. They had to be seated at table when the gong sounded. One of David's fellow guests at Rock Hall, Edward Hodgkin, has given an account of the cultural strenuousness and the many intolerances that informed life in Helen Sutherland's house:

> Visitors were expected to join in all activities arranged for their benefit, whether this was a long walk in the hills, reading Wordsworth aloud after dinner, going to church, or listening to a recital of music. At all times you were expected to pull your weight with intelligent conversation. You were not expected to bring muddy shoes into the house, to make loud noises, to ask for special favours in the way of food and drink, to read *The Times* before she did, to sleep with your bedroom window shut, or to stay up after your hostess had decided it was time to go to bed.[3]

Helen Sutherland was endlessly generous to David but when she died in 1966, leaving him £5000 in her will, he remarked at the time 'she'll push them around in Heaven quite a bit'.[4]

In the spring of 1930, a few months after his first visit to Rock, David shared an exhibition with Ivon Hitchens, a fellow member of the 7 and 5 Society, at the Mansard Gallery Annexe at Heal's in Tottenham Court Road. It was a great success both in terms of sales and critical reception. For instance the art critic of *The Times*, in a review of the show published in the paper on 13 May 1930, concluded that 'There is no living artist with a style that may more fairly be called "lyrical" than that of Mr. David Jones.' The reviewer singled out *Montes et Omnes Colles*, the painting which David had done whilst with the Cleverdons at Lourdes. *The Times* critic thought that 'his "Montes et Omnes Colles" is as praiseful as one ever saw, fairly singing its way about the page'.

In these very productive years he showed a wide range of paintings at a succession of exhibitions. His work was shown in the galleries of prestigious art dealers such as Tooth's, the Leicester Galleries, the Beaux Arts and Wertheim. In January 1931 he was well represented at the 7 and 5 Exhibition and in November of that year at the Lefevre Gallery. Three months later, in February 1932, there was another 7 and 5 Exhibition. It was David's greatest success so far. He sold more than any other artist participating. A few months later, in March, there came another important development in his rapidly burgeoning career. For the first time a selection of his work was put on public exhibition in America. Curators from the Art Institute of Chicago invited him to contribute some of his paintings to their *Twelfth International Exhibition of Water Colours, Pastels, Drawings and Monotypes*. Other artists represented in the exhibition were Oskar Kokoschka, Henry Moore, Christopher Wood and Raoul Dufy. The same institution was also mounting a show entitled *First International Exhibition of Etching and Engraving*. To this too David loaned some examples of his work and his engravings for the *Ancient Mariner* were also on sale at the gallery.

David's paintings made their way slowly into North American collections, but it is the case that his paintings and engravings did not have the same impact on the North American art world as his literary works have had upon the world of letters on the other side of the Atlantic. *In Parenthesis* in particular has compelled the attention of numerous critics and scholars in the United States and Canada.

An achievement that made 1932 an especially memorable one for David was the virtual completion of the manuscript of *In Parenthesis*. He had begun the book about four years previously by writing captions for some drawings he had done of soldiers in the trenches of the First World War. There developed a continuity between the captions, they gradually became his prime concern. They evolved into a narrative while the illustrations were disregarded. By the time the book was finished a front piece and an end piece were all that was left of them.

When he first began the writing, David worked secretively, sometimes to the irritation of his father. To check facts he made visits to the Imperial War Museum and consulted a trench map of the Mametz Wood sector. David was much stimulated by, and the documentary side of *In Parenthesis* much assisted by, a book that was published in 1930. This was *Up to Mametz* by Wyn Griffith, who had been a young company officer in the battalion in which David served. This book was very influential on the documentary aspect of *In Parenthesis*, and describes the same series of military events in 1916 that are covered in David's book.

David wrote a good deal of his book during his early visits to Rock Hall, and the writing was finally completed at Pigotts in August 1932. All the time he wrote, he continued to paint producing a profusion of portraits, animal paintings, interiors, still lifes, landscapes and seascapes. It is highly likely that this hectic activity was one of the causes of the breakdown that afflicted him in 1932. It came soon after the completion of *In Parenthesis* and prevented him from going on to take the necessary steps to find a publisher. Several painful years of inactivity lay ahead and not until 1936 was he sufficiently recovered to be able to put some extra finishing touches to the book and submit it for publication.

8

Depression Years
1932–6

DAVID REMEMBERED THE ONSET of his breakdown vividly. He had been on an extended stay with his parents at Brockley. ('That was a mistake,' he told an interviewer nearly forty years later.)[1] Suddenly he was stricken by a terrible insomnia: he would lie in bed and hear the clock strike every quarter of every hour throughout the night. Then he would get up and 'shaved and dressed like a normal human being' would go downstairs. Very evidently the surreal feeling that he was not 'a normal human being' intensified his fear of his condition. The insomnia continued day after day.

Early in 1933 he set off for Pigotts. René Hague was now living there, married to his long-time sweetheart, Eric Gill's daughter Joan (or Joanna). David was given a small bedroom through which the married couple had to pass in order to reach their own bedroom. This, together with some of David's habits and the need to live so close together, irritated Joan but René was more sympathetic. He has described how the breakdown developed at Pigotts at this time, quoting some of David's own expressions of frustration. The illness showed itself, he writes, in 'an increasing quietness, a brooding, outward signs in language and behaviour of an exasperated bafflement: "I can't work . . . the whole thing's a monumental bollux, a first-class buggeration".[2]

What David found most agonizing in his situation was his unprecedented inability to paint. Only if he refrained from working was his condition at all assuaged, but then he was tortured by months of the 'misery of enforced and frustrating idleness'. His breakdown has been attributed to several causes: to sexual difficulties, to social uneasiness as he moved in the world of Prudence Pelham (he was much intimidated by her mother Lady Chichester), and to years of overwork. He himself saw part of the cause as something to do with his problems as an artist. Writing to Jim Ede about a series of watercolours painted in 1932 just before his breakdown – *Still Life with Plate and Goblet, Briar Cup, The Table, Still Life* and *July Change, Flowers on a Table*, all of which are clearly attempts to present still-lifes sacramentally – he observes 'that the 1932 group got nearest to what I had in mind – but *a very long way from the goal*. (I suppose that may partly explain my complete crash – I was conscious for some long time before it came that I was straining every nerve to do something more than I had power to do).' Jonathan Miles and Derek Shiel have agreed with this and have convincingly identified the nature of the failure with greater explicitness: 'His Expressionistic watercolours of this period reveal him wrestling with internal disruption and discontent and the more meditative pictures reveal his proximity to the moment of vision. But although these large watercolours promise a moment out of time, a look beyond the mundane and gross, we do not quite catch "heaven in a wild flower" which is the aspiration of the mystic. These watercolours hover on the frontier and refuse to echo deeply like sublime music or the conundrum of a mystical writing. They move, transfixing with their beauty, yet leave the spectator on the brink.'[3]

Early in 1934 Tom Burns made up his mind that David had to be helped. His brother, Dr Charles Burns, had put David in touch with Dr Woods, a neurologist who specialized in nervous disorders associated with shell-shock, but so far David's condition had not improved. He continued to be depressed and frightened, he could not paint, and he had come to the point at which he had nothing he could offer for sale and had become virtually dependent on the financial support of Helen Sutherland. Now it was that Tom Burns hit on the idea of a sea voyage to the Middle East as a way of taking David out of himself and helping him to recuperate. David was fearful about going but Tom Burns persisted. He made all the arrangements and paid for everything.

They embarked on a P&O boat moored in the Pool of London, very much Eb Bradshaw country. They sailed down the Channel and around the Bay of Biscay which, fortunately, was not stormy. In his letter to David in his autobiography, Tom Burns recalled how the voyage brought some improvement in David's health. He also remembered an incident that was typical of David's illness.

. . . you found immense relief in the cabin comfort and the positive and immediate devotion of your Goanese steward. By the time we reached Gibraltar you had been often out on deck and were greeting other passengers but the idea of boarding a lighter with the rest of them to visit Gibraltar was too much for you. When the last of the lighters had left there were a few dinghies bobbing about and calling for custom. 'Come on, let's go,' you suddenly said, so off we went at much greater discomfort and expense than all the other passengers. But you had made a leap into reality – away from the 'heebie-jeebies' and 'Rosie' as I used to call your neurotic 'come-overs'.[4]

When in the Mediterranean David and Tom played deck-tennis. Tom took a photograph of his friend on board ship at this time, which shows David lounging against a companionway, a cigarette between his lips with a long stretch of ash carelessly unremoved. He is wearing large baggy trousers, a dark jacket and a light shirt with a high collar and loosely knotted tie. He has a floppy white hat and heavy dark-rimmed spectacles. There is a certain ambiguity in his pose and it is, as in portrait photography generally in those days, very much a pose. His stare directed away from the camera can be seen to express the dreamy melancholy of someone who is depressed and self-absorbed, but as the eyes behind the spectacles ponder distances his attitude may also be seen as that of the *contemplateur* and the artist. For all his psychological illness and his tormenting incapacity as an artist his stance here suggests that he has not given up on this definition of himself.

The two companions arrived in Cairo where they spent some days with friends. Then came David's first experience of travelling in an aeroplane, when he flew on to Lydda in what was then the British Protectorate of Palestine. From there he went on by car to Jerusalem and joined Eric Gill at the Austrian Hospice there. Gill was in Jerusalem to complete some decorative panels for the New Archaeological Museum. One day, looking out from his bedroom window in the Hospice, David saw Eric Gill coming down the street, stop by a leprous beggar who was sitting in the gutter and drop a coin in his bowl and kiss him. Also staying at the Hospice was Thomas Hodgkin, whom David had first met at Helen Sutherland's home. Hodgkin was now on the staff of the British Governor of Palestine.

The weather in Jerusalem was extremely hot. To Eric Gill's disgust, David insisted on remaining inside his room, reading Trollope's *Barchester Towers*. In a letter to Saunders Lewis in April 1971, he recollected that 'I hardly moved out of the Holy City, but used to watch from my window which faced south, with the Mount of Olives on my left and east, and the "Mosque of Omar" in the middle distance and the tangle of meandering streets from immediately below and stretching away to the west.'[5] Occasionally, when the heat lessened, he did venture out. He remembered how he used 'to meander about the densely crowded and incredibly noisy streets and the Suq – chaps on donkeys or mules – Palestinian Arabs in ceaseless argument over the price of anything and everything from a melon to a tin kettle – (the colour of brass but seemingly the most skilfully contrived out of discarded petrol tins).'[6]

He did visit Bethlehem and found it very beautiful. From one of his conversations with David, William Blissett reports that 'One day a masterful man on the spot arranged for them to go to the Church of the Holy Sepulchre, but David, to the other's shocked annoyance, said, "No, I think I'll stay right here and have a double scotch". He never did see it. Either you can take a sight or you can't, and there's no use pretending.'[7]

But there was one unanticipated sight that came David's way in Palestine that did have a great impact on him, and that was the British troops who policed the streets wearing the uniforms and using the slang of soldiers he remembered from the First World War. The sight set him thinking; he was intrigued to think of soldiers from the British imperial order, serving in Palestine. He went on to ponder the possibility of soldiers of the Roman imperial order, serving in Palestine at the time of Christ, being posted to Britain. It is a historical antithesis that he considers and dramatizes at some length in his later poems.

All in all, though, the visit to Palestine was not a success. For one thing he was in considerable physical distress. Thomas Hodgkin, who saw David often during his visit, wrote in a letter that David came 'against his will under the pressure of friends who thought that they knew what was good for him, and is wretched and grows wretcheder as the heat grows intense'.[8] In another letter Hodgkin is more specific about David's discomfort: 'Egypt has given him mosquito bites as big as billiard balls and perpetual stomach ache – he can eat little – loathes the hospice food . . . He is a stone lighter and naturally troubled by his lightness. He does look ill, but then he always did.'[9] David himself confirmed that his trip to the Middle East had not helped him. In a letter of July 1934, written as he prepared to return to England, he wrote that 'I don't think it's done much good. It's all too exhausting.'[10]

Back in England later that year, 'Rosie', to use Tom Burns's euphemism, returned. The uncured depression was aggravated by the shocking realization that for the first time since he had exhibited with the 7 and 5 Society six years before, he had nothing to send to that year's show. As the year moved towards its end his misery grew. He seems to have reached a point at which he could not stand to be in London and to be aware of the competitive London art world in which he was no longer able to participate. As Christmas approached he set off for North Devon in the company of the ever-solicitous and would-be helpful Tom Burns. They spent the holiday at Hartland Point, the wild and remote western headland of Bideford Bay, some seventeen miles from the town of Bideford itself. Quay Hotel, where they stayed, stood high on the cliffs looking out over a cold blustering sea on which, over the centuries, countless ships had been wrecked on the rocks beneath. David and Tom Burns stayed at Hartland Point for a week. David thought the hotel 'horribly expensive' and his spirits did not improve. Tom Burns recalled that a 'knowing friend' had told them that Quay Hotel 'might be guaranteed not to have the slightest hint of the commercialized Christmas from which we were in flight. It was a lovely spot indeed but we came down to dinner to find two paper hats on our dinner table.'[11]

In the New Year of 1935 David moved down to the South Devon coast and began the first of his many extended stays in Sidmouth, a small seaside resort with a Victorian esplanade. He settled into a room in the Fort Hotel and used it as his base for several years to come. It was the first of a series of single rooms which for the rest of his life would constitute his home, or his 'dug-out', as, using a phrase particular to the First World War, he often called it.

Harman Grisewood, on his first visit to David in his Devon retreat, found the Fort Hotel extremely ugly but David insisted that it was *very* comfortable'. Tom Burns also came, dashing down from London in his Wolsey Hornet for a weekend in Sidmouth. He was somewhat surprised to find David chatting to elderly ladies and retired colonels in the hotel, but when there came a pause in these conversations David would whisper to Tom 'Let's go for a wet' and they were off to the nearby pub for a pint.[12]

Prudence Pelham also came to visit David and shared Harman Grisewood's distaste for the hotel. Using the racy language that matched David's own she mocked the Fort Hotel's 'bugger of a salon by the lobster fireplace'. She also disliked Sidmouth itself with its 'lioness-coloured sea' and its 'loathly red cliffs'.[13] But David clung to his bolthole and found that as long as he remained 'in hiding' in Sidmouth his mental condition remained not too bad. Whereas, if he ventured into London, it deteriorated quickly.

Prudence's visits to David in Sidmouth could sometimes be fraught with tension and upset. Once, after she had returned home, she wrote him a letter in which she sought passionately to repair an unhappiness she had caused. (At one point she calls him Dai, a name used only by those who were closest to him.) She writes:

> So very dearest David most darling David – how short it was – I did hate leaving you – I did not say it a lot because I knew I would have to go and you did not want me to . . . *I did love* being with you, you do know that don't you? Things will come better I do believe. There are a lot of things I would write but it is not much good to write complicated personal things in a letter I think – it leaves the other person under a barrage of words. Be very safe my darling Dai . . . Good night my sweet David please please be happy I can't bear it when you are miserable and I have made it worse.[14]

But they did have happy times together. On one occasion they had an excursion from Sidmouth to the nearby village of Ottery St Mary, just a few miles to the north. Here they shared together a great pleasure and excitement at the ancient parish church of honey-coloured sandstone, standing picturesquely on the banks of the little River Otter. David was greatly taken by an effigy of a medieval knight, and Prudence enthusiastically supported him in his idea that a picture of the effigy could be used as one of the illustrations in *In Parenthesis*. (In the event this was not done.)

By the spring of 1936 David's spirits started to revive. He did some simple watercolours of Sidmouth and felt able to take up the manuscript of *In Parenthesis* again. But he was not very confident or positive about it. In March he told Jim Ede in a letter that he was 'working on the typescript of my book' but found it 'terribly bad in places – in most places in fact'. He did add, however, 'but I'm incapable now of forming a judgment'.[15] But despite his despondency he persevered with the job of revising the manuscript and later in the year he sent it to Faber and Faber, who accepted it for publication.

David's editor at Faber was Richard de la Mare, son of the poet Walter de la Mare. He agreed that René Hague, who now ran a small, professional printing press, should have the contract to print *In Parenthesis*. However, de la Mare thought René and David out of their minds when they proposed that the book should be published as a 'crown folio, 10 by 15 inches, with two columns of 12 pt Joanne and a headline (just PART 4) in Gill Sans Bold caps'. René Hague conceded that though this format 'looked grand', it was 'not very practical'.[16]

In Parenthesis was announced in Faber's spring list for 1937. A letter to Jim Ede conveys something of David's excitement at seeing his book advertised, even if he did find the blurb 'embarrassing'. It pleased him too that in this same publisher's list there was also announced René Hague's translation of the *Chanson de Roland*, a work to which reference is movingly made in *In Parenthesis*. In June 1937 David's book was published in a print run of 1500 copies. It was a historic moment in literary history. A first work and a masterpiece, it is one of the eight great works that constitute the pre-eminent achievement of British modernism in the thirty-year period in literature which began with the serialization of *Ulysses* in *The Little Review* during the First World War and ended with T. S. Eliot's completion of his *Four Quartets* in the early years of the

Second World War. (The other five major modernists texts are Hugh MacDiarmid's *A Drunk Man Looks At The Thistle*, Eliot's *The Waste Land*, Joyce's *Finnegans Wake* and D. H. Lawrence's *The Rainbow* and *Women in Love*.) Like these works, *In Parenthesis* is not for casual reading; it makes demands upon the reader and can be difficult. But it is also richly rewarding. In the following chapter I will try to characterize the special verbal achievement and the high literary art that is contained in *In Parenthesis*.

9

In Parenthesis
1937

A CHRONOLOGICAL NARRATIVE WRITTEN IN opulent, intricate, highly poetic English, *In Parenthesis* consists of seven parts. The first details the parading of 'B' Company, made up mainly of Welshmen and Cockneys prior to their marching off to one of the south coast ports from which they sail to France. After disembarking they are taken in cattle trucks towards the front. The time is December 1915 – 'late in the second year' of the First World War. The omniscient narrator often focuses on John Ball, the awkward, clumsy private, who is the central character of a book that presents, and sometimes just names, very many soldiers. *In Parenthesis* gives us a strong sense of a group, a collectivity, as well as of individuals.

The second part shows the Company training behind the lines and then moving closer to the front, puzzled then intrigued by the increasingly damaged landscape along their way. The first shocking confirmation of their closeness to the fighting comes when John Ball, in the act of lending matches to his officer, Lieutenant Jenkins, hears a German shell hurtling towards him. The two last paragraphs of this section which describe the devastating explosion, are cinematic and vivid aurally as well as visually.

Part 3 describes the Company's long and wearying march into the trenches. It is night-time and sometimes they are in cloud and rain and sometimes in moonlight. The section is a fine prose poem about light. It concludes with a weary John Ball, put on sentry duty, culpably drifting off to sleep.

The fourth section describes trench life from dawn to dusk; it shows mundane activities such as the soldiers' uncomfortable, unsatisfactory breakfasting and the cleaning of rifles. The fourth section is also the central section of seven and at its centre is an extended poem which is of major thematic importance: this is the boast of the Welsh soldier Dai, who wears a 'misfit outsize greatcoat' which associates him with a character from Malory's, *Morte D'Arthur*, Dai de la Cote male taile. David's footnote to the passage shows his awareness of the boast as a long-established verbal and literary convention. And Dai Greatcoat's boast is a great *tour de force*: it celebrates Wales as a more ancient culture than England and proclaims conflict and war as the eternal conditions of the universe. Dai, identifying himself as the perennial, archetypal soldier during various stages of history claims, at the end of his five-page-long boast, that 'I was in Michael's trench when bright Lucifer bulged his primal salient out.'

The fifth part begins in the *estaminet* or bar to the rear of the trenches. The soldier's conversation is full of differing and conflicting rumours. The Company is marched off, then turned around and marched back. The grand old Duke of York is remembered. But finally the Company is moved into the position from which they will participate in the attack on the German-controlled wood. 'Now in this hollow between the hills was their place of rendezvous.'

The sixth part begins with a period of watching and waiting. John Ball has time to visit and to converse with his close friends Signaller Olivier and Reggie, one of the Lewis gunners. On the following day, in the rainy afternoon, they see for the first time infantry going forward to assault.

In the seventh and final part 'B' Company itself goes forward to join in the attack on the wood. One after the other they are killed or wounded. John Ball is among the latter, being shot in the leg. He crawls painfully away at the feet of his advancing comrades. He drags his rifle which is metaphorized as a woman, a beloved, a wife. When, in his increasing weakness, he finally feels compelled to abandon it he experiences a sad resignation in the loss of soldier-liness, even of manhood. The last three lines of the section, which are taken from René Hague's translation of the *Chanson de Roland*, movingly declare a relationship between John Ball and the author of *In Parenthesis*.

One function of the name 'John Ball' is to associate this book with one by a writer who was as important to David Jones as he was to Eric Gill. The writer is William Morris whose *A Dream of John Ball* published in 1888, is thematically very similar to *In Parenthesis*. The central theme in both is fellowship. Both books celebrate and commemorate it. Morris's John Ball is the priest turned revolutionary who was one of the leaders of the Peasants' Revolt in 1381. As he and his followers – clearly analogues for Morris and his fellow socialists of late Victorian England – fight for their egalitarian beliefs before ultimately undergoing capture and execution, Morris's John Ball often preaches the value of comradeship and fellowship. The following passage from *A Dream of John Ball* could easily apply to David's commemoration of 'B' Company and the sense of fellowship within it:

. . . forsooth I knew once more that he who doeth well in fellowship, and because of fellowship, shall not fail though he seem to fail today, but in days hereafter shall he and his work yet be alive, and men be holpen by them . . .[1]

A few pages earlier, Morris's John Ball speaks even more insistently about the importance of fellowship:

Forsooth, brothers, fellowship is heaven, and lack of fellowship is hell: fellowship is life and lack of fellowship is death: and the deeds that ye do upon the earth, it is for fellowship's sake that ye do them, and the life that is in it, that shall live on and on for ever, and each one of you part of it, while many a man's life upon the earth from the earth shall wane.[2]

In Parenthesis carefully particularizes the fellowship that exists within 'B' Company. It takes many forms: it shows in the shared humour that is sometimes ironic, sometimes foul-mouthed, sometimes Cockney, sometimes Welsh; it is there in the solidarity that the men feel in their scorn for the generals and senior officers at headquarters; it is there in the group moods that David so delicately evokes: suspense, tiredness, frustration, fear; and it is there in a host of tiny incidents. For instance, Private Saunders and two comrades have built a bivouac against the rain with their ground-sheets. Saunders is suddenly ordered elsewhere and takes his with him. The other two are surprisingly upset by his departure and the loss of their new-made home. 'For such breakings away and dissolving of comradeship and token of division are cause of great anguish when men sense how they stand so perilous and transitory in this world.'[3] The style here is that of Malory, one of the many voices that tell the story of 'B' Company. More devastating than the bivouac incident for the group is the prospect of going into the attack on the wood with little hope of returning alive. The soldier who expresses the pessimism of the Company uses a mixture of Malory and modern colloquial English, saying 'how it was going to be a first clarst bollocks and murthering of Christian men and reckoned how he'd throw in his mit an' be no party to this so-called frontal-attack never for no threat nor entreaty, for now, he says, blubbin' they reckon, is this noble fellowship wholly mischiefed.'[4]

Some of the phrases in the lengthy and moving dedication confirm David's intention to commemorate the fellowship he had known and which helped to redeem the horrors of that terrible war: 'THIS WRITING IS FOR MY FRIENDS . . . AND TO THE MEMORY OF THOSE WITH ME . . .' *In Parenthesis* is a homage to male bonding in the most painful and horrific of circumstances. But it is also about women, the feminine and the female. The women remind us of another, more normal and routine life than that being lived by the soldiers. As 'B' Company sets off for the wasteland of the trenches, 'a place of enchantment' as David calls it in his Preface, Miss Veronica Best and her helper, Violet, who run the refreshment hut at the military training camp in southern England, are concerned only with the practicalities of supplying food. Alice, the waitress in the *estaminet* in France and, unlike the proprietor Jacques, pro-English, busies herself serving drinks and finds the war lucrative rather than in any way disturbing. Visually, Alice is presented in one of the several similes from painting in the book: 'her rounded elbows lifted, as Boucher liked them'.[5]

To the soldiers, memories of their womenfolk back at home are a solace. A Warwick subaltern snuggles in the comforter his girl has knitted for him. 'The precious: she's made it of double warp.' He imagines her knitting it in Stretton after she and her family had left Tite Street in Chelsea because of the Zeppelin raids. Cockney soldiers think sensuously, tactilely, of their girls working on the stalls in the London street markets, girls 'whose burgeoning is finery trickt out, who go queenly in soiled velveteen, piled puce with the lights' glancing'. And the Jewish soldier, who is among the first killed, in the final section 'cries out for Deborah his bride'.

Women are important in the intricate mythological context within which David situates his account of the First World War. In his boast Dai pays a special tribute to Helen Camulodunum who, as a footnote informs us, was 'a majestic figure out of the shadows of the last ages in Roman Britain'. A legendary figure thought to be the daughter of Coel Hên, the supposed founder of Colchester, she was a great inspirer and leader of men. 'She's clement and loving, she's Friday's child, she's loving and giving'; Dai is proud to claim to have served under her.

Women also supply important mythological metaphors in a book that is extremely rich in metaphor. The terrible massacre in the final section is presented as the work of 'sweet sister death' who on this day has turned herself into a repugnant whore. She 'has gone debauched today and stalks on this high ground with strumpet confidence, makes no coy veiling of her appetite but leers from you to me with all her parts discovered'.[6] And at the last, as so many of the soldiers lie dead among the trees of the wood, the near-delirious John Ball has a vision of the 'Queen of the Woods' adorning them with branches, boughs, flowers and berries. And it is to the Virgin Mary that a prayer is addressed as the few surviving members of 'B' Company face the hail of German bullets. The prayer has a stylistic shift in the final line quoted that is characteristic of David's verbal procedures in *In Parenthesis*:

> Maiden of the digged places
> > let our cry come unto thee.
> *Mam*, moder, mother of me
> Mother of Christ under the tree
> reduce our dimensional vulnerability to the minimum—[7]

The female figures having to do with the world of divinities are part of one of the major strategies of the book – that is, to remind us continually of the epic and the heroic in Western literature. Certainly in one respect *In Parenthesis* is a documentary giving us a very realistic account of the First World War. One readily understands why Colin Hughes, in an important essay in the history of David Jones' scholarship, '*David Jones: The man Who was On The Field* subtitled his piece '*In Parenthesis as Straight Reporting.*' The book is very much a product of the 1930s when reportage or documentary emerged as an important aesthetic principle. It is there, for instance, in the documentary films of John Grierson and in George Orwell's books of reportage such as *The Road to Wigan Pier* and *Down and Out in Paris and London.* Yet there is vastly more to *In Parenthesis* than its documentary reporting. This kind of writing alternates with passages that refer to, or are quotations from, works of heroic literature such as the *Chanson de Roland*, the Old Testament histories, *Y Gododdin*, the Welsh poem about another, more ancient, disastrous military expedition, and Shakespeare's play about heroism with a prominent Welsh component, *Henry V.*

Here is an example of the heroic style, typically full of allusions, and prosodically and in lineation in vers libre, to

which the narrator switches as he reports the final destruction of 'B' Company, as the men

> sink limply to a heap
> nourish a lesser category of being
> like those other who fructify the land
> like Tristram
> Lamorak de Galis
> Alisand le Orphelin
> Beaumains who was youngest
> or all of them in shaft-shade
> at strait Thermopylae
> or the sweet brothers Balin and Balan
> embraced beneath their single monument.
>   Jonathan my lovely one
> on Gelboe mountain
> and the young man Absalom.
> White Hart transfixed in his dark lodge.
> Peredur of steel arms
> and he who with intention took grass of that field to be for
> him the Species of Bread.
>   Taillefer the maker
> and on the same day
> thirty thousand other ranks.
> And in the country of Béarn—Oliver
> and all the rest — so many without memento
> beneath the tumuli on the high hills
> and under the harvest places.[8]

The sounds of lament and compassion here are characteristic of the final part, and indeed of the book as a
whole, and contribute to its emotional impact upon the
reader. The documentary writing particularizes the terrible
here and now. The passages in heroic style put this present

into a larger perspective in time and history. Such a conceptualizing aids the work of redemption which *In Parenthesis* undertakes. War is a perennial part of the human condition, the implication runs, and war brings suffering and agony. But these experiences may be redeemed by the experience of fellowship and also by creating the work of art that testifies to fellowship. In succeeding in precisely this ambitious literary task, David Jones created a great and noble book.

10

The Attractions of Adolf Hitler
1937–9

Around the time of the publication of *In Parenthesis* David was greatly pleased to have some of his paintings included in the British contribution to the Venice Biennale of 1937. This must have been some compensation to him for the setbacks in his career as a painter in the previous year. Members of the 7 and 5 Society had to be re-elected annually and at the March meeting David, who received only two votes was excluded from the Society. This must surely have been a blow, although in a letter to Jim Ede he claimed not to care: 'What a pity I did not send in my dignified letter of resignation a year ago – but in a way it's much nicer to be hoofed out.'[1] David was probably voted out because he had contributed little or nothing to the group over the past few years. In addition, under the powerful influence of Ben Nicholson, the Society had become increasingly committed to abstract painting and sculpture, whereas David never wavered in his commitment to representational art. But this division and his rejection by his former colleagues meant that he was cut off from one of the most vital and innovative groups in British art in the 1930s. For all his nonchalance in writing to Jim

Ede he must surely have felt this exclusion as a bitter loss.

He experienced another, more painful loss in 1937 when his mother died. With her gone he no longer used the house in Brockley as one of the several homes to which he travelled. When he needed to be in London he would stay with Jim and Helen Ede in Hampstead or with Charles Burns in Chelsea. It is clear there was no rift between David and his widowed father; indeed until his father died six years later he was always solicitous about him and paid him regular visits. But it would seem that after his mother's death, the house in Howson Road no longer had the appeal of a home for him. Meanwhile David was especially grateful for the hospitality of Jim Ede, and reflecting later upon his illness he wrote: 'I do so often look back on the days I used to come so frequently to Hampstead and laugh with you round the fire. I do not think I could have stood those years without coming.'[2]

The month in which that letter was written, November 1936, was the time of the mounting climax of the abdication crisis in which King Edward VIII found himself as a result of his involvement with the American divorcée, Mrs Wallis Simpson. Despite the Catholic view of divorce, David – always chivalric and royalist – was a passionate supporter of the King and an opponent of the Prime Minister, Stanley Baldwin, and the Anglican establishment which would not tolerate the King's marriage to the woman he said he loved. One of David's very many stories about the First World War had to do with his brief meeting with the then Prince of Wales.

In the Great War, the boyish prince often used to duck his equerries, snag a bicycle, and pedal off towards the front line. His remark that his father had other sons is often remembered. One day, Private David Jones was shaving and, he recalls, wearing a particularly tattered 'weskit', when a boyish figure appears and says 'Hello, which way to A Trench, Boesinghe sector,' and, being told, heads off. Winded pursuers, retired Guards officers recalled to duty, red-faced and big-moustached, rush in and very improperly demand, 'Have you seen Wales?' 'Yes, sir.' 'Why didn't you stop him?' 'How could I, sir?' And really, how could a half-shaved private soldier be expected to sequester the heir apparent?[3]

Twenty years later that private soldier had become a public figure. He was fortunate in having so many friends who worked to promote his reputation, Jim Ede being one of them.

In 1938 Jim Ede set off for the United States to embark on a nationwide lecture tour. He made a point of showing slides of David's paintings and did all he could to boost David's reputation there. It seems likely that it was due to Jim Ede's influence and enthusiastic advocacy that in the following year examples of David's work were included in the art exhibition at the New York World's Fair. David's literary reputation also received a boost in 1938 when he was awarded the Hawthornden prize for *In Parenthesis*. The award was presented to him in the offices of the National Book League in Piccadilly. Many of his friends from Pigotts attended the presentation. Barbara Wall, herself a resident at Pigotts, remembered how the distinctive clothing of the members of the community stood out in that sophisticated West End context: 'There was a great gathering of hand-woven suits and terracotta ties in the sleek premises of the National Book League . . .'[4]

Another accolade, though a rather unsettling one, was the praise for *In Parenthesis* from the Irish Nobel laureate

W. B. Yeats. David, together with Prudence Pelham, was at a tea party given by her mother, Lady Chichester, in her London home. The tall figure of Yeats appeared at the door of the drawing room. His great mass of white hair was swept back and he wore an elegant light-coloured suit and the blue shirt which formed part of the uniform of the followers of the Irish Fascist leader, Eoin O'Duffy. Yeats scanned the room, which by now had fallen silent. At last he spotted David, came over to him, bowed flamboyantly and declared in ringing tones: 'I salute the author of *In Parenthesis*.' He then proceeded to praise the book lavishly and at great length. David felt shy, did not know how to respond to what was being said and was much embarrassed by the occasion.

This was one of the last outings together of David and Prudence. A few months later, early in 1939, David was staying in Sidmouth when he received the staggering news that Prudence Pelham had married. Her husband was someone she had known for many years, a school friend of her brother. David wrote of his shock and upset in a letter to Jim Ede:

> I love her very much and our friendship has meant everything to me. So naturally, however much this may be a 'good thing', I've naturally had a twisting, trying to get all the tangled delicate emotional bits and pieces tied up and sorted out ... She is such a marvellous and unique, truly intelligent, and beautiful person ... we were so alike in lots of ways. So naturally a change in her life of so fundamental a character requires in me a readjustment ...[5]

In the event Prudence's marriage did not mean the end of her friendship with David. They continued on kindly terms, exchanging Christmas and birthday presents for many years.

The year 1939 brought another kind of ending in David's life. Helen Sutherland's lease of Rock Hall had run out and she moved to Cockley Moor in Cumberland, near Ullswater in the Lake District. Cockley Moor, an estate of some two hundred acres up in the hills, was close to the small village of Dockray. The house had formerly been a farm and Helen Sutherland employed Sir Lesley Martin, the future chief architect to the London County Council and Professor of Architecture at Cambridge, to refurbish the property. He thoroughly modernized the place and installed very large windows so that the wonderful views of the surrounding countryside were made visible. But for all the attractions of Helen's new home, Rock Hall was a loss to David. He loved the area's historical associations, especially with the Roman Empire; he was particularly attracted to Hadrian's Wall because, as he said in a letter, 'one feels the presence of the Legions in a most extraordinary way, perhaps because one can see its alignment for miles going over rises in the hills and dipping out of sight'. The place gave him, he wrote to another correspondent, 'the feeling of the past living in the present'.[6]

However, there was more to David's life during this period than loss and melancholy. There was, for instance, the extraordinary escapade of his breaking into and burgling the Italian Consulate in London with his friends Tom Burns and Harman Grisewood. The latter recalled the episode almost forty-five years later in a letter to Thomas Dilworth. The three friends, he remembered, had been out to dinner together (perhaps it had been quite a vinous dinner); they were walking home through Mayfair when they noticed the Italian Consulate looking very deserted. By the late 1930s, Grisewood observed, he and his friends had come to think of Mussolini, the Italian Duce, as 'a somewhat absurd Opera Buffo character'. The three of them clambered over the area railings of the Consulate and broke into the building. Going through the empty rooms they found a large stack of writing paper, each sheet bearing the letterhead: 'Il Ministro della Cultura Popolare. Appunto per Il Duce'. They decided that friends of theirs would be either entertained or shocked to receive letters on such stationery, so they stole a considerable amount of it. Harman Grisewood concedes that such behaviour might have seemed out of character for David Jones but insists that David enjoyed the exploit as much as his two friends did. In later years David used some of his share of the Fascist notepaper for some early drafts of passages of what would become *The Anathemata*.

Fascism, German more than Italian, was a major concern for David in the years immediately prior to the Second World War. Unquestionably he felt sympathy for Germany, for National Socialism and for Hitler. Others in his circle shared such views. Tom Burns, for instance, wrote of 'those darkest years just before the war. They were dark indeed. Munich, of course, proved to be an illusory hope, but the vociferous opponents of the settlement filled us with despair. There were those who were looking forward in every sense to war: bridling, truculent, offensive, arrogant and in deadly earnest. Churchill was their prophet. They took delight in his defiance of all diplomatic endeavour to avert the catastrophe. I had many dissident German Catholic friends, exiles all. We would meet regularly but with little comfort beyond the belief that Europe would not commit suicide. But it did.'[7]

David was also a supporter of the British government's policy of appeasement, which was being so forcefully denounced by Winston Churchill. David's pro-German feelings went back to the First World War; he had clearly had great respect for the German soldiers against whom he had had to fight. Among those to whom *In Parenthesis* is dedicated are: 'the enemy front-fighters who shared our pains against whom we found ourselves by misadventure.' Just before Christmas 1938 David sent a copy of the book to the Prime Minister, Neville Chamberlain, whom he greatly admired. In an accompanying letter to Chamberlain, recently returned from his Munich meeting with Hitler, David wrote of how he and his British comrades in the trenches had looked forward to a day when they could become friends with the soldiers on the other side. He greatly regretted that this 'instinctive aspiration and one natural to soldiers' had been frustrated by subsequent events.

David Jones had certain things in common with Hitler. They had both known combat in the First World War. Both had fought in Mametz Wood, though at different times, and both had received leg wounds there and been evacuated to a field hospital. In *Mein Kampf* Hitler reports how in the field hospital he awoke to hear the voice of a German woman, the first such voice he had heard in two years of military service. The incident is remarkably similar to David's long remembered and cherished experience of hearing the voice of an aristocratic English nurse when he came round in the field hospital after himself being wounded and then falling unconscious.

Earlier in the 1930s David had read *Mein Kampf* in what he called a 'miserable "cut about" edition'. But in October 1938 he was reading the book in a complete version. He told Harman Grisewood that he was 'deeply impressed by it'.[8] But he also had reservations. For though he did 'like a lot' of what Hitler wrote, he also found that 'this *hate* thing mars his whole thing'. Nevertheless David was sufficiently engaged by Hitler's critique of capitalism and of the Western democracies that he devoted a long essay of some twenty foolscap pages, typed and double-spaced, to an examination of it. Copies of the typescript are lodged in the Burns Library at Boston College. Thomas Dilworth, in his judicious essay 'David Jones and Fascism', quotes a considerable amount from the manuscript.

David begins by acknowledging the similarity between some of Hitler's social criticism and that of many Catholic intellectuals. They too were concerned 'to free men from the many and great evils of "capitalist exploitation" ', to help them 'to live uncorrupted by the "banking system" ' and 'to effect some real and just relationship between the price of things and the labour expended'.[9] They too were concerned 'about the exploitation of the citizen . . . alien financial control, lands going to waste'. 'What it all boils down to "he deduces" is that there is much in both the Fascist and Nazi revolutions that demands our understanding and sympathy.'

He cautions against British criticism of German expansionism. He stresses the fact of British imperialism: 'our ancestors . . . gathered the world's wealth . . . by the application of armed and economic pressure . . .' it took a lot of gangster-work and breaking of heads and hearts to rear the stately homes of England'. He adds self-deprecatingly: 'and you have to have a fairly large police force, I imagine, before it is possible for a neurotic aesthete, like myself, to exist at all'.[10]

Should Britain go to war with Germany, he continues, 'it will not be an affair of morals or the defence of civilization but simply a "struggle for survival" for both parties.' He deplores the reception given by the British press and politicians to the speeches of Hitler, who 'has always protested, as clearly as a man could, his desire "to be our friend" ',

David sees hostility to Germany as a tragedy. 'By a sort of alchemy of prejudice and fear every word and every deed, good, bad or indifferent, coming from the supposed enemy is transmuted into a base thing.' David is in no doubt about what he must do: 'To question and mistrust the work of such alchemists is surely our duty.'[11]

These views, which David was by no means alone in taking, have been made by history to appear naïve and misguided, if not wicked. At the end of the war, as the extent of Nazi atrocities became clear, he realized his error. A friend reports him saying quite simply: 'I got that Nazi thing wrong.'[12]

But in 1938, in a review of his friend René Hague's translation of the *Chanson de Roland*, David gave some indication that he believed that Hitler might succeed in taking over Europe. In his review, published in *The Tablet* and entitled 'The Roland Epic and Ourselves' he gives ample praise to his friend's book. He writes that René Hague as a:

translator has succeeded, because of his own true poetic intuition (which has enabled his use of an exact, simple, evocative word-relationship) in rendering into modern English prose an ancient French metrical work, and absolutely to convince us of the poetry of the original. He uses no archaisms, no tricks, no artificial means, to convey the metre and rhythm, yet he makes us feel the kind of composition the original is – how it belongs to that time when a poem was made essentially to be declaimed to an assembly. It is to be hoped that he will find it possible to translate other *chansons de geste*.

It should be pointed out that this edition of the *Roland* is unique in the history of such attempts – for the translator is also the printer. His work as a printer is too well known for it to be necessary to speak of the excellence of the typography of this book. If he should serve as a model to translators, he should serve equally as a model to printers. It is a book which in every way deserves to be widely known.[13]

In the review, along with praise for its author, David also involves himself in lengthy speculations about literary and cultural history, and here it is that he suggests that Hitler may well come to control Europe. Britain and Germany are compared with other historical dualities in which an older order was superseded by a new one:

> It is, conceivably for a baptized Führership that we may yet have cause to pray, if only in the sense that a sophisticated Roman of the Province would have asked heaven's prevenience for the difficult barbarian invested with The Purple; or a Celtic Christian might, just conceivably have prayed for Edwin, with his assumed insignia of the *Dux Britanniarum*.[14]

David's sense of profound tragedy as war with Germany approached had a very distinct effect upon his art. In his painting, as he had done in *In Parenthesis*, he sought to contextualize the situation confronting him by employing larger and more mythological references. He took up some very ambitious subjects rich in religious, cultural and art historical connotation. In 1938 he began doing sketches for the large watercolour *Aphrodite in Aulis*, which was the first of these 'big subject' paintings. Now in the Tate Gallery, the work was virtually completed two years later in 1940 and signed in 1941.

The title recalls the story of how Agamemnon, leading

his Greek army to war, made up his mind to sacrifice his daughter Iphigenia to obtain the favourable wind his fleet needed for him to proceed with his military mission. The sacrificial figure at the centre of David's painting is not Iphigenia but rather the goddess of love. She is, as Paul Hills has suggested in a lengthy account of the painting, both an object of worship and a victim of sacrifice. The historical context which makes her a figure of sacrifice is established by the two figures on either side of her, creating a configuration suggesting a crucifixion. Below her to her left stands a youthful British soldier and to her right a young German. This is love shown in the time of twentieth-century war. The expression on the face of the goddess is pensive, sad, resigned, even grim. David once said that in this painting he had turned Aphrodite into 'a nice girl'. The reductiveness seems to be greater than that. He shows her as a deformed figure with heavy unshapely legs, a thick tubular neck, plump cheeks and a balding brow. Behind her are numerous smaller figures all involved in hectic, frantic action. The painting is about chaotic disorder and, centrally, loss. In the background is a classical, semi-circular screen of columns with different capitals, the two on the left looking primitive and unGrecian. The damage to the screen suggests a ravaged world and reinforces the theme of the destruction of beauty. The plinth on which the disfigured Aphrodite stands is being boarded up by the British soldier with a piece of the corrugated metal much used in the manufacture of underground air-raid shelters during the war.

In the same year that he began this painting David was also working on a new and similarly ambitious literary project. He entitled it 'The Book of Balaam's Ass'. Never completed, it is a work, as we have it printed in *The Roman Quarry* edited by Harman Grisewood and René Hague,

115

consisting of twenty-four pages in which the first five and the last nine deal with the subject of the creaturely and the creation. The destruction that took place in the First World War is the subject of the middle section of some eight pages. This begins with an account of an attack on a German stronghold on the Somme known as 'the windmill'. The section starts with a description of the structure given in the technical and objective language of military reporting, but soon we move into a lengthy and rhetorical passage, listing the names and indicating the characters of the British soldiers who try to advance upon this windmill, struggling over barbed wire without an iota of cover. 'There was no help for them either on that open plain because the virtue of the land was perished and there was not grass but only broken earth and low foliage of iron.'[15] The plain covered by the German guns had 'not a bush, no brick-hot, not any advantageous fold, no lie of dead ground the length of a body . . .'[16] The names of the entirely unconcealed soldiers proceeding dutifully to their deaths are accompanied by memories of, and some anecdotes about them.

Horrifically, on the barbed wire ahead of them, hang the limbs and the bodies of the Irish troops who had mounted an attack on the windmill on an earlier occasion, in the autumn of 1915. Before that, in the early summer, yet another British assault had been repulsed with appalling loss of life – only three soldiers surviving. These were Private Lucifer, Private Austin and Private Shenkin. The first two names are blatantly symbolic. The first is that of the devil, the second an abbreviation of that of a saint, St Augustine. The third, Private Shenkin, David once acknowledged, is a self-portrait. Shenkin is known to his section as 'Pick-em-up Shenkin', the nickname echoing the presumably often repeated order addressed to him by the drill sergeant on account of his slovenly marching. Shenkin is forgetful, sleepy and clumsy. But it is his physical mal-adroitness that makes him one of the three survivors. As his comrades are killed around him he stumbles into a shallow crater and lies there until dark when he leaps back to the assembly trench. Though a survivor, he is an abject figure who has known 'the baptism by cowardice which is more terrible than that of water or blood'.

That the survivors constitute a trinity of sanctity, devilry and weak humanity relates the realistic war narrative to the large and complex mythological concerns that dominate this poem in prose. It is a work which in opulent, vivid language accepts and praises the whole of creation. The biblical phrase that supplies the title to the work indicates a prime authorial insistence. As Balaam's ass in the Book of Numbers was, unlike his master, aware of and responsive to the presence of God, so animals in this work are shown to have an awareness of God's patrimony. For instance, the cow has 'the tormenting buzz of memory – the bovine race-myth',[17] the wolf has 'his grey beauty flaming',[18] the owl has her proverbial wisdom even though she is one of the predators in God's Creation. Predatoriness, like devilry, is for David a part of 'the fantastic hierarchy', whose only order we can seem to figure out is:

> this blood for that life
> this pain for that wholeness
> moon-toil for this ebb . . .[19]

The penultimate section of 'Balaam's Ass' presents a contrast to the grandeur of creation evoked earlier. It is a satirical account of what David calls the 'Zone', which on one level is the modern materialistic and utilitarian world and on another the training ground near Winchester where David trained before embarking for France. It is a place of sterile rituals full of complacent and blimpish voices. The satire is cut short as David turns to describe his personal quest for God's creaturely world in a civilization made up of an ever-increasing number of manufactured articles, gadgets and materials. 'I have felt for his wounds in nozzles and containers.' 'I have been on my guard not to condemn the unfamiliar.' But finally he is unable to find the creaturely in townscapes dominated by the kind of 1930s modernist buildings created by Walter Gropius and Mies van der Rohe. 'I have said to the perfected steel: be my sister, and to the glassy towers: Bend your beauty to my desire.' 'But my hands found the glazed-work unrefined . . .' 'I have howled at the foot of the glass tower.'[20] This painful failure is probably one of the main reasons David finally abandoned this work, disparaging it in a letter of May 1938 as 'a rambling affair about ideas'.[21]

David also began other literary projects at the end of the 1930s. None of these manuscripts was completed at the time and the history of subsequent redactions of and additions to them in the later years is extremely complicated, as René Hague and Harman Grisewood point out in *The Roman Quarry*, in which some of them appear. One of David's literary undertakings just before the Second World War was the first of his 'Mass' poems, works which, while relating the details of the celebration of the Mass, also evoke historical, mythological and literary associations of various words and phrases spoken by the celebrant. These early 'Mass' poems are trial versions of *The Anathemata*. Of them it could be observed, as David said of his second book-length poem: 'You can go around the world and back again, in and out of the meanders, down the history paths, survey *religio* and *superstitio*, call back many yesterdays, but yesterday week ago, or long, long ago, note Miss

Weston's last year's Lutetian trimmings and the Roman laticlave on the Deacon's Dalmation tunic, and a lot besides, during those few seconds taken by the presbyter to move from the Epistle to the Gospel side, or while he leans to kiss the board or stone (where are the tokens of the departed) or when he turns to incite the living *plebs* to assist him.'[22]

From now until the end of his writing career the 'Mass' poems would continue as one of David's chief concerns. 'The Kensington Mass' and 'The Grail Mass' are printed in *The Roman Quarry* in versions that date from later in David's life.

His first mention of a 'Mass' poem came in January 1939 when he told Harman Grisewood in a letter that 'I'm absorbed in my Absalom Mass, part now'. One passage to do with Absalom appears as the last three paragraphs, all in prose, of 'The Kensington Mass'. David uses Absalom – 'this young man of singular beauty of princely blood loved by all the people, fair of aspect and his golden tresses excelling his sister's whom he greatly loved'[23] – as an analogue for Christ. Riding under a 'vast oak', Absalom gets caught in its branches and is suspended there until killed by his enemies. Like Christ he dies hanging from a tree.

Another Absalom passage appears in 'The Old Quarry', which is also a Mass poem. Lineated as poetry, it reads in part:

> his gilte tresses clere
> the younger one that was pierced
> whose white sockets the oak-boughs bruised
> whose ivory belly they blemished with iron
> so that you wouldn't regard him.[24]

'The Old Quarry' is a 'Mass' poem that meditates on the present as well as on the past. There are numerous allusions to the political situation in Europe in 1939. David speaks of the Reich, of 'the führer of the north,'[25] and in what is surely a kindly meant phrase, of the '*Volk* consanguine'.[26]

On the day the Second World War began David was at Pigotts. After he and his friends learned that the British ultimatum to Germany had been ignored there was great excitement. Barbara Wall remembered. David was involved in intense discussions about the implications of the declaration of war, and doubtless felt great consternation and regret. But ironically, in the event, the period 1939 to 1945 proved to be for him a time of considerable personal achievement and success.

11

The War Years
1939–45

DURING THE FIRST YEAR of the war David spent more and more of his time in London. On the day France surrendered to the Germans he had been taken to hospital in Sidmouth with acute appendicitis. A priest stayed with him during and after the operation. After his recovery in that June of 1940 he left his room in Sidmouth for the last time, shortly after completing the watercolour, *Promenading at Sidmouth*. It is painted in delicate pastel colours with numerous small figures reminiscent of those in the paintings of L. S. Lowry. At first, in London, he divided his time between the Chelsea homes of two of his friends, that of Harman Grisewood in the King's Road and that of Tom Burns in Glebe Place. But in the middle of the Blitz on London in 1940 Grisewood got married and moved with his bride to an eighteenth-century cottage on the banks of the Thames at Richmond. So Glebe Place became David's only residence. He remained there and took care of the place when Tom Burns was required to go to Spain on a diplomatic mission.

During this year of the Blitz David's career as a painter began to pick up again. In January there opened an exhibition of twenty-five of his watercolours at the Redfern Gallery. Both reviews and sales were excellent. The director of the Redfern, Rex Nan Kivell, was delighted with David's success and continued to give him shows throughout the war years and beyond. Later in 1940 examples of his work also formed part of a major exhibition at the National Gallery entitled 'British Art Since Whistler'. At this time he also completed the first of the three large and complex watercolours which preoccupied him during the early years of the war, works vastly more ambitious than *Promenading at Sidmouth*.

The first of them, from 1940, was entitled *Guenever* and depicts an event described in Malory's *Morte d'Arthur*, Book XIX, Chapter 6, in which Launcelot tears the iron bars of a window from a wall in his determination to break in upon King Arthur's Queen. On the right of the picture the helmeted Launcelot is shown as a wrenched, twisted figure. One of David's subjects in this work is desire as agony. The violence of Launcelot's entry and the tortured contortions of his body caused by his obsessive love contrast with the calm of the rest of the painting in which the luminous, naked queen sleeps serenely, surrounded by her slumbering attendants. (Some of the attendants at the foot of the painting are reminiscent of those in Henry Moore's shelter drawings showing Londoners sleeping alongside each other on the platforms of tube stations during the Blitz, drawings which David greatly admired.) Except for the leaping cat, which Launcelot has disturbed and awakened, the human and animal figures all lie still. But the building in which they rest, shown as a chapel in the top left of the picture, and as a domestic interior with a large pot over a fire at the bottom right, looks architecturally unstable and precarious. It is a rocked and shaken building such as David would have seen during the bombing of

London. But the deeper meaning has to do with an experience of sexuality well understood by David; it shows the effect that Launcelot's violent penetration of the place has upon this sacred and domestic interior. The painting is thus a meditation upon the way in which female beauty creates desire and in which desire – tormented desire – responds to beauty.

In an essay published in November 1940 at the height of the Blitz David pondered the notion of beauty. The essay he found 'not an easy task' for it was an obituary published in *The Tablet* for his old friend and sustainer, Eric Gill, who had died that month. David's attitude is admiring, grateful and affectionate, but he is in no doubt about the differences between Eric Gill's career and his own. Gill was a workman, a craftsman, but David recognizes that he himself belongs with artists, and with a particular group of artists. In words that constitute an important act of self-definition, albeit inspired by the loss of Eric Gill, he writes: 'In spite of the disavowals of the aestheticism of the nineties, we are, far more than is generally recognized, inheritors of a not very dissimilar "philosophy of art", we are still "of the decadence", however robust and "primitive" some of our expression has been. It has remained an exasperated search for beauty on the part of individual men conscious or unconscious of the declining West. Here Picasso and the rest and all the lesser of us are tossed on the same sea as Beardsley . . .'[1] But Eric Gill was not of this company.

In a carefully considered and balanced assessment of Gill's career, David concludes that his carvings of inscriptions were his greatest achievement. 'One thing is certain: as a carver of inscriptions he stands supreme. There the workman scaled the heights of pure form, and some of his inscribed stones possess the anonymous and inevitable quality we associate with the works of the great civilizations, where an almost frightening technical skill, for a rare moment, is the free instrument of the highest sensitivity – and the Word is made Stone.'[2]

But although David's agenda, he now realizes, was different from that of the workmanlike Eric, he missed him greatly. He continued to visit Pigotts from time to time to see the surviving members of the Gill community but found it 'strange with dear Eric no longer at the helm.'[3]

Within days of Eric Gill's death in November 1940, Britain suffered a colossal air attack that was dramatic and devastating. Given by the Germans the mocking code-name *Mondlicht Sonate* (Moonlight Sonata) it was a massive raid on Coventry involving in the region of 440 aircraft of the Luftwaffe. Coventry city centre and the medieval cathedral were virtually destroyed and nearly 600 people were killed on that one night. The horror had a profound effect upon David. He thought about it a great deal during the weeks following the raid and over the Christmas period and then in early January 1941 produced a painting which he datelined 'Epiphany 1941'. At the bottom of the picture he quoted words from the Coventry carol, 'O sisters two what may we do'.

The painting, now in the Imperial War Museum, is called *Sisters Two* but is also known as *Britannia and Germania Embracing*. It shows two helmeted women with long tresses holding each other uncertainly. The armour they wear distorts their femininity just as the war, the iconography of the painting implies, distorts both Britain and Germany. Britannia's helmet has monstrous protuberances like a stag's antlers made of metal. The foliage on her arm looks either like camouflage or an ugly tattoo. With tense talon-like hands and fingers Britannia and Germania reach out to embrace each other. It is a moment of recognition; the two figures are illuminated by the star of the Epiphany.

But they stand before a devastated, burning landscape and a seascape in which images of pain and suffering abound. Animals bay, a spire tumbles down from a church in flames, a ship is sunk. The searching expressions which Britannia and Germania direct into each other's eyes convey a profound sadness, helplessness and hopelessness. Their yearning is the emotional centre of a work that is otherwise almost simplistically emblematic. The painting transcends the likely emotions, after the attack on Coventry, of anger and grief. Like T. S. Eliot at the end of the third section of *Little Gidding* – itself, in great part, a poem about the German bombing of London – Jones is compassionate towards both Germany and Britain. He shows them, as Eliot did his Royalists and Cromwellians in the last war that damaged the fabric of Britain three centuries before, accepting 'the constitution of silence'.

Later in 1941 David completed another ambitious work, entitled *The Four Queens*, and like *Guenever* illustrates an incident from Malory's *Morte d'Arthur*. Four queens approach a recumbent Launcelot, competing for his love. The four female faces that are the focal point of the picture all have different expressions. The lady on the left maintains a sidelong, thoughtful gaze; her companion to the left also gazes, but suspiciously and intently. The figure third from the left has a twisted mouth and a faraway look, and the lady on the extreme right stares rather anxiously, looking mesmerized. That the painting is a study of different modes of womanhood is clear enough, but some of the detailing – which is very extensive – is enigmatic and puzzling. Like other paintings from the early 1940s, *The Four Queens* clearly demands to be 'read' but it is not easily construed. Why is Launcelot's helmet like that of a German soldier? Why are his feet placed upon his dog like those of a knight on a Renaissance alabaster table-tomb? In Malory Launcelot merely sleeps, but in this painting there is a suggestion that it is a dead man lying under the heavily fruited apple tree, a branch of which curls about his planted lance. His inert body contrasts with the several highly energized horses that are in motion in the painting. Yet dead or incapacitated or sleeping Launcelot has been susceptible to the power of the four women, even though they do not look directly at him. All five figures are suspended in a trance of sexual expectation.

The Tate Gallery purchased this painting and also '*Guenever*'. Nevertheless David's financial position was precarious as it so often was throughout his life. Finally he had to acknowledge that he could not afford the upkeep of the house at Glebe Place and in October 1941, at the time of the German siege of Leningrad, he moved into a boarding house at 12 Sheffield Terrace, just off Kensington Church Street. He hoped to be there only temporarily but in the event this proved to be his home until after the war. Here he had but a single room and his meals were brought up to him on a tray. The enforced move there from Chelsea he described in a letter as 'a ghastly blow'. His room he said, was 'bloody small and dark'. He pinned a large map of North Wales to the wall. Ominously, after he had completed *The Four Queens* his insomnia started to recur.

A month after he had moved to Sheffield Terrace he was required to register for Industrial Service, a government programme that directed civilians into work that contributed to what was called the war effort. David failed the medical examination outright. The doctor who examined him reported:

In 1932 he had a nervous breakdown and developed symptoms of mental depression – a depressive psychosis. The condition was severe. The course has been

126

marked by improvement with relapses. He has been unfit for consecutive work in his own profession for nearly ten years. He is unstable, and under stress of duty would relapse. He is, in my opinion, quite unfit for routine service.[4]

So David returned to his one-room home where he persevered with his painting and writing.

David's widower father had also been forced to move; he had developed a serious heart condition and could no longer manage the house at Brockley. He gave it up and moved into a nursing home at Sydenham. Brockley was badly bombed in the Blitz, and the night after night air-raids were the cause, David believed, of the deterioration in his father's health. Yet he also recalled that when the raids were actually going on, his now eighty-two-year-old father 'did not turn a hair'. David visited his father in the nursing home once a week and spent most of the day with him there. To be near his father was for him an important reason for staying in London.

Except for his trips to Sydenham David never left central London for about two years. But in August 1942, at the time of the great battle for Stalingrad, he went up to Pigotts to celebrate Petra Tegetmeier's birthday. He intended to go just for the day but was persuaded to stay for a week. He found Petra and her two blonde daughters were looking very beautiful.

In wartime London David had a busy social life. He came to know more and more people in the world of the arts. He met Ben Nicholson again and found him more human than when they had last met around the time of David's exclusion from the 7 and 5 Society. He lunched with his fellow Catholic writer, Graham Greene and saw T. S. Eliot and attended Eliot's 'long lecture' on Virgil. David also met and became friendly with Kenneth Clark (later Lord Clark), who had been appointed Director of the National Gallery in 1934, when he was only thirty years old and who continued in that post during the war. He was the author of many books on art and from the 1940s on was a leading commentator on art in the media of radio and television. David found him 'awfully nice', 'awfully understanding and able at the same time'. 'He is doing a *great* work in England under war conditions for the arts.'[5] Clark was handsome, urbane and very wealthy. Socially well-connected and extremely influential in the London art world, Clark undoubtedly assisted David's career and reputation greatly at this time. Clark was a friend of the then Queen (later the Queen Mother) and it seems highly probable that it was he who interested her in purchasing some of David's paintings. Clark was also the general editor of a series of books entitled 'Penguin Modern Painters' in which he included a volume on David Jones. This particular volume Clark entrusted to the editorship of Robin Ironside, who worked for the Contemporary Arts Society. David greatly liked his editor when they met in 1942 to begin working together on this first book, or perhaps monograph on David's art. Its publication was long delayed; it finally appeared in 1949.

David's literary activity also continued during the early years of the war. Though he was having great difficulties with 'The Book of Balaam's Ass', he did successfully complete some major essays during this period. In 1941 he wrote 'Religion and the Muses', in 1942 'The Myth of Arthur'; and in 1943, the year in which his father died, 'Art in Relation to War.'

The first essay – 'Religion and the Muses' – tackles a subject to which David as essayist frequently returns, his non-modernist (and non-postmodernist view) that technology and what he often calls the 'utile' dominate the modern world and in so doing make the possibilities for art extremely difficult. 'Today we live in a world where the symbolic life (the life of the true cultures, of "institutional" religion, and of *all artists*, in the last resort – however much we may discover the association) is progressively eliminated – the technician is master.' Artists, he concludes, 'are all very like men forced into guerrilla tactics – we operate in a terrain over-run by the enemy – and pretty efficiently administered by him'.

'The Myth of Arthur', which runs to some forty-eight pages, first appeared in a volume that was a Festschrift for the Catholic writer Hilaire Belloc which was brought out by the Catholic publishing house, Sheed and Ward, in 1942. The essay begins by considering the history of the Arthur stories which were so important to David both for his writing and his painting. With his considerable learning worn very lightly, David shows how 'so strangely does myth plus legend plus history weave its meander'.[6] Towards the middle of the essay he digresses and contemplates his own times. He observes that 'From the rise of Romance literature until just recently, the love interest has dominated the field in all our story-telling; there are signs that the tide is turning – both in literature and in life. The war of cultures and ideologies has returned, our individual passions are already taking a modified position in relation to affairs of race and myth and idea.' The author of *In Parenthesis* adds: 'Perhaps we are entering again upon a period when the love story may give place to the story of the heroic and of heroics – both.'[7] But he immediately goes on to say that 'It is to be hoped that this masculine influence is at all events tempered by the saving scepticism of the female mind; there is a danger of Juno being put into a concentration camp, of her being liquidated.' David adds that 'The male principle, which is seen in Fascism now, is always fighting the female principle, which has found its way into Communism, and lost much of itself as it went.'[8]

The second half of the essay is taken up for the most part with quotations from, and an appreciation of, Malory's *Morte d'Arthur*, one of the most significant works of literature for David Jones. He is a great admirer of Malory's literary skills, saying of his book that 'whether grave, gay, profane or sacred, of the contingent or the absolute, all is held within the restraint of an extremely economical, deceptively simple, native English prose style'.[9] This sentence is a good example, in vocabulary and in phrasing, of David's capacity for making very careful and precise formulations as a literary critic.

'Art in Relation to War' is another substantial wartime essay; it is more than forty pages long. It is an important part of that tradition of thought concerning art and society that we associate with William Morris and Eric Gill. David begins by establishing a very expansive notion of art. (He was always much taken by the statement attributed to James Joyce that '"art" comprehends all our activities from boat-building to poetry'.) Early in 'Art in Relation to War' David reminds us that there exists the phrase, 'the art of war'. In a footnote he recalls how Winston Churchill paid tribute to General Rommel's African strategy, a gesture, he adds, that was 'resented by ignoble minds in this country'. For David 'the art of war is capable, at all events, of a form-creating quality', and goes on to say that 'not only Norman vaulting, not only Piero della Francesca's *Nativity* but Rommel's desert tactic and Nelson's Nile touch, are empty of all significance – "they need not have bothered," unless form is good in itself.'[10]

In David's view there is an artist – actual or potential – in everyone, but contemporary society represses this in people through 'the full sub-humanization of Industry'. 'In the sphere of art, conditions can arise where the men of a whole culture are made eunuchs, owing to the particular demands that utility and materiality, profit and power may make within that culture . . . And that is the kind of deprivation which the conditions of our kind of age seems to impose upon great numbers of people, upon most people. This deprivation is, in the sphere of art, analogous to a sterilization or a castration in the physical sphere.'[11]

It seems likely that the recent death of Eric Gill to some extent motivated David in the writing of this essay, in the middle of the war. A phrase from Gill is repeated and celebrated throughout the essay. It is cognate with David's own notion of the gratuitousness, the non-ideological nature of art. The phrase is there at the end of the question that is at the centre of the essay: 'How, we ask ourselves, given on the one hand the nature of man, and on the other hand the conditions of the age, and the rapid intensification of those conditions in the future, can man fulfil himself with respect to what Eric Gill, with his genius for precision, termed "the one intransitive activity" of which man is capable?'[12]

Early in the war CEMA (the Committee for the Encouragement of Music and the Arts) had been founded thanks to a grant from the Pilgrim Trust. The Committee would later become the Arts Council of Great Britain. Kenneth Clark became chairman of the CEMA art panel and under its auspices arranged in 1944 for an exhibition devoted entirely to David's work to tour the country. It was well attended and well reviewed in provincial newspapers.

David, meanwhile still had money worries, and in the summer of 1944 Jim Ede came up with a scheme to co-ordinate the financial support given to David by his various friends. On 9 August 1944 David, who was staying at

Pigotts with René and Joan Hague, wrote to thank him. He clearly felt a little uneasy about accepting the money and also uncertain how to express his gratitude. 'I hope I do right in accepting what you've planned – I feel very un-generous and careless in the face of this generosity.'[13]

'The Book of Balaam's Ass' continued to be a problem for him but in this same year there was an important new development in David's practice as an artist. He began to work on lettering and on the making, that is to say the painting, of inscriptions. As Nicolete Gray has remarked, his 'inscriptions were a means of conveying his manifold layers of meaning in visual terms.' Just as passages in his literary work refer to works in Latin, Welsh, Old English, Middle English and other languages, so the lettering in his inscriptions may be made up of characters that are Greek, Roman, Early Christian or Anglo-Saxon. The first impor-tant inscription from this time was completed in 1945 and consists of a sentence taken from the Anna Livia Plurabelle section of James Joyce's *Finnegans Wake*. David had ad-mired this book ever since René Hague had read him passages from it some time in the early 1930s. One sentence appealed to him greatly and is quoted and referred to several times in his own writings. It is but five words long: 'Northmen's thing made southfolk's place'. For David the statement expressed the historical continuity that was so important to him; the sentence speaks of 'the change of people on the unchanged site',[14] and speaks of how one phase in the history of settlement and civilization contains within it relics and artefacts of preceding phases. David's inscription of the sentence was done with water colour, pencil and wax crayon, rubbed on so as to make the letters look as if they are incisions in ancient worn stone.

However, not all David's lettering was employed to elaborate upon venerable truths. A familiar object in wartime Britain was the rather ugly, bureaucratic ration book issued to every man, woman and child by the Ministry of Food. It contained the coupons necessary to buy supplies. Evidently David could not tolerate the look of his ration book and covered it with lettering, ending with a phrase in Latin, 'Ubi est tritium et vinum'. The book is now in the National Library of Wales.

In April 1945, as VE day approached, David's work was shown in an exhibition shared by contemporary French and British artists which marked the reopening of the St George's Gallery in the West End of London. The artist and critic Michael Ayrton, writing in *The Spectator*, found David's painting *Fuchsia Hedges* to be 'superb', 'the most exciting exhibit'.

Just over a month later there was a general election in Britain, in which the Prime Minister Winston Churchill, leading the Conservative Party, was massively defeated and replaced by the Labour leader, Clement Attlee. David voted Conservative even though he rather admired Attlee and 'was consolable when he beat Churchill in the election of 1945'.[15] And he 'spoke with warm admiration of Aneurin Bevan',[16] the eloquent Welshman who was the Labour member from the Rhondda Valley and who was to pilot through the House of Commons the legislation that created the National Health Service.

In November 1945 David was one of 'Nine British Contemporaries', an exhibition that was shown in Paris at the British Council galleries in the Champs Elysées. The opening was a grand occasion with many distinguished figures from the art world of the day attending, including the critic Herbert Read, the sculptors Henry Moore and Constantine Brancusi, and the painter Georges Braque. In the early postwar years David's work would be an important part of other similar exhibitions designed to promote

British art abroad. He may have lived in a tiny room in a shabby boarding house in Sheffield Terrace and been poor and in precarious health, but by the end of the war he was indisputably established as a leading figure in contemporary British painting.

12

Illness and Achievement
1946–52

IN THE FIRST YEAR after the war David went up to Cumberland to stay with Helen Sutherland at her house, Cockley Moor, in the Lake District. In a letter of 23 August 1946 he described the setting of the house as 'wild and remote' but the interior had 'all Helen's civilized feeling just as Rock had'.[1] He especially admired Helen's collection of Ben Nicholson's paintings. A fellow guest at Cockley Moor that month was Kathleen Raine, a poet who would become an important commentator on, and propagandist for David's work. David read aloud passages from what would become *The Anathemata* to Kathleen and Helen. Having now abandoned 'The Book of Balaam's Ass'; and this new project was his principal literary concern. He reported that the ladies at Cockley Moor seemed to like what he read 'quite a bit', but, he conceded, 'I'm afraid it's damned obscure'.[2]

David also painted during his stay with Helen Sutherland, or at least he tried to, telling one correspondent, 'I've been trying to paint with conspicuous unsuccess.'[3] He was endeavouring to paint landscapes seen from his bedroom window, but as most of his recent painting had either been

135

inscriptions or figurative-cum-emblematic pieces, he felt 'rusty' trying to paint the landscape of Cumbria. Nevertheless he did complete four fine view paintings: *The Hogget, Helen's Gate, Above the Aire Beck* and *The Legion's Ridge*. This last title alludes to an old Roman road on the far side of Ullswater and is another instance of David's concern to view the land of Britain in terms of Roman remains, to show it as part of the empire to which the land of Jesus Christ also belonged. Miles and Shiel point out, convincingly, that David's enhancing of the hills in the middle distance in *The Legion's Ridge* 'suggests anthromorphism, as if a sleeper is laid out beneath a sheet'.[4] The suggestion is of a sleeping lord, a *rex quondam futurusque*, a Christ figure who will one day return. Writing to Helen Sutherland after his return to London, David remarked of the paintings he had done during his stay with her 'Don't know what I think about them – you can see *something* in some of them and then it goes again – rather boring'.[5]

His uneasiness and dissatisfaction with his paintings may well have been one of the causes of the terrible setback that afflicted David during his stay in Cumberland. He had a second major nervous breakdown, which this time took the form of uncontrollable fits of fright and panic. He managed to return to London but bouts of illness recurred, with a particularly bad attack occurring in November 1946. That month the BBC broadcast a radio version of *In Parenthesis* which David listened to. According to Douglas Cleverdon, in his essay 'David Jones and Broadcasting', the 'vivid externalization of the horrors of trench warfare'[6] in the programme precipitated a state of breakdown in David that lasted for several weeks.

The New Year did not bring a full recovery, and by the spring of 1947 his condition was so bad again that he was forced to enter a nursing home. Dr Charles Burns, brother of David's friend Tom Burns, arranged for him to stay at Dr Hugh Crichton Miller's clinic at Bowden House in Harrow-on-the-Hill. Here he was treated by Dr Bill Stevenson, a trained Freudian analyst. In the mid-1930s Dr Woods, who had attended David during his first breakdown, had taken the view that if painting caused David to be ill he should cease painting and 'cultivate a masterly inactivity'. But now, at Harrow, Dr Stevenson took a different approach: David should paint and conquer the illness that painting had seemingly precipitated. He told David: 'You must have been a bloody sight more frightened in the First World War than you realized at the time.'[7] Dr. Stevenson, whom David came very much to like and admire, engaged in regular sessions of psychotherapy with him in which he also probed his patient's sexual malaise. David complied with his doctor's request that he try to write down his own thoughts about his difficulties in this aspect of his life. Dr Stevenson also encouraged David to have periods of rest and relaxation, to do gardening and to participate in ball games with other patients at the clinic. In addition, he was also given tranquillizing and sedating drugs and underwent the crude electric shock treatment in use at that time.

Gradually, very gradually, Dr Stevenson's regime proved successful and after six months David was able to leave Bowden House in January 1948. His stay there had been extremely expensive and he was now in great financial difficulties. His bills were paid for the most part by Helen Sutherland. He also received a small grant from the Artists' Benevolent Fund to which he had made application. Anxious to earn some money David arranged to have an exhibition of his work at the Redfern Gallery in May and June 1948. He was now well enough to work at new paintings for the show. He also had some in hand. For during his time in Bowden House he had painted a number of pictures. From his window in the nursing home he had had a view of the many trees in the large garden. Trees now became his subject.

Trees at Bowden House is one of the early paintings in the sequence; it is a simple representation in an Impressionist manner of five trees. As the sequence continues David gives to his pictures of trees titles that require us to see philosophical and religious implications in them. The titles are taken from the Anna Livia Plurabelle section of James Joyce's *Finnegans Wake*: *My Branches Lofty*, *The Dusk is Growing* and *Tys Elvenland*. This last title – made up of the Danish words for 'hush' and 'small river' and the Dutch word *Elvenland*, meaning 'fairyland' – underscores the quiet and mysterious intensity of the picture. The tree here is painted in such a way as to recall the Cross of Christ. *Tys Elvenland* prepares us for *Vexilla Regis* (The Banner of the King), a tree painting which also shows a reversion to David's emblematic mode.

Vexilla Regis refers to a Latin hymn that alludes to the legend that the blood of Christ transformed the dead, rootless wood of the Cross into a living tree. The painting was bought by Jim Ede for his mother, and in a letter to her David gave some account of the extensive symbolism of the work. The subject was 'the collapse of the Roman world'.

The three trees as it were left standing on Calvary . . . The leopard's pelt and trumpet in the left-hand bottom corner are supposed to be the instrument and insignia of a Roman bucinator or trumpeter, as though the owner of them had been part of the guard on Calvary . . . The tree on the left . . . is, as it were, the tree of the 'good thief', it grows firmly in the ground and the Pelican has made her nest and feeds her young, in its branches – Our Lord is likened to a pelican in her piety in one of the Latin hymns of Thomas Aquinas. The tree on the right is that of the other thief, it is partly tree and partly triumphal column and partly imperial standard – a power symbol, it is partly supported by wedges. St. Augustine's remark that 'empire is a great robbery' influenced me here.'[8]

In the spring of 1948 David painted hectically in order to increase his offerings for the coming exhibition at the Redfern Gallery. After leaving the nursing home he had remained in Harrow because he still needed to have a weekly consultation with Dr Stevenson. He moved into a single room in a boarding-house on Peterborough Hill, very close to Harrow School. This was Northwick Park Lodge, a large and imposing Victorian house built of grey brick and with a portico. The proprietor was Christopher Carlisle, a former master at Harrow School. David got on well with him and admired him but was saddened to witness a growing drinking problem. Some years later Carlisle could regularly be seen stumbling drunkenly around the house, bottle in hand.

A convention at Northwick Park Lodge was that the residents took their evening meals together in the dining-room. Some of David's fellow lodgers were single masters from Harrow School and the remainder were all people of some education, though one or two of them were now living in reduced circumstances. David did not enjoy the greasy food served at the Lodge, but in compensation the conversation over dinner was usually lively and erudite. In the dining-room there was an *Encyclopaedia Britannica* which the residents used to help settle matters on which they disagreed. One history master from Harrow School, Geoffrey Treasure, recalled how eager David was to converse about Wales, Bede and post-Roman Britain.

David's room was on the third floor. It was quite large and bright and had large sash-windows. From here David could look out over the garden, an orchard and nearby playing-fields, towards London in the distance. He soon became very fond of his 'high-perched room in that rambling, ill-kept, but "creaturely" house,' and from his windows he resumed his painting of trees. In contrast, his paintings were now no longer emblematic in the way they were just before his breakdown. *Tree at Northwick Park*, for instance, is a vibrant expression of his sense of the life in the tree, with the meaning and power of the painting all in the colour, line and texture.

In 1948 David's paintings appeared in exhibitions in Vienna and Austria, but by far the most important to him was that at the Redfern Gallery for which he had so energetically prepared. On show were thirty-two of his works, twenty-six of which had been done at Bowden House or Northwick Park Lodge. But for all his recent efforts the show did not renew or re-establish his reputation as he had hoped. He was disappointed by the reviews as they began to appear in the press in June, and was particularly upset by the comments from his fellow artist Wyndham Lewis, whom he had once, in Lewis's Vorticist period, very much admired. Lewis disparaged David's paintings at the Redfern as 'characteristic water-colours representing a fairy-book world'. David told Helen Sutherland that he found the 'lack of perception on the part of the people who ought to see deeper very depressing'.[9]

And yet, if art critics were not enthusiastic about his paintings, purchasers were. The tree pictures sold well, *Tys Elvenland*, one of the Joyce-inspired paintings, sold for £125 as did *Mr. Carlisle's Acacia*, which went to an

Australian buyer. The records of the Redfern Gallery indicate that total sales, after the deduction of commission, amounted to more than £1,800. But David himself claimed to have received far less. To a correspondent he grumbled that after paying tax and dealing with his general expenses he was left with very little indeed.

Later that year examples of his work formed an exhibition entitled 'Contemporary British Drawings' held at the British Council gallery in Ottawa. And the following year, 1949, he was included in 'Contemporary British Art' at the New Burlington Gallery. This was the year in which Robin Ironside's monograph on David finally appeared. Part of the Penguin Modern Painters series, edited by the then Sir Kenneth Clark, it comprises thirty-two plates and a sixteen-page introduction, which is mainly biographical.

In the late 1940s and early 1950s David was quite active as a book reviewer, chiefly for *The Tablet* and *The Dublin Review*. Perhaps this was to help ease his financial difficulties. However some of the reviews from this time are of sufficient substance that Harman Grisewood saw fit to include them in *Epoch and Artist*, the collection of David's prose, which he brought out with David's co-operation in 1959. In April, 1950 David reviewed Bernard Berenson's *Aesthetics and History*. The review gave him an opportunity to sketch out his own views on art. He is respectful towards Berenson, who had been Kenneth Clark's mentor at I Tatti near Florence; Berenson is 'the learned and perceptive author'. But David quickly distances himself from Berenson's insistence that, with very few exceptions, European art is 'Mediterranean', founded in the Hellenic period and renewed in the Renaissance in Italy, with all subsequent art of any value deriving from it. David cannot agree with the famous connoisseur that regional cultures are 'peripheral'. He goes on, 'When further we read . . . the words "flaccid puerilities and crudities" to describe, for example, certain phases of Coptic, Saxon and Merovingian art, we see how deep those disagreements may be. One begins to wonder what might be the verdict upon those marvellously virile abstract forms which the Celts of the La Tène culture contrived partly from the Mediterranean motifs.'[10]

Also in 1950 David reviewed a book about James Joyce's Dublin. This enabled him to praise an artist whom together with Picasso he rated most highly among his near contemporaries. Joyce was also ammunition to be used against the likes of Berenson. For Joyce and his work were very much of one provincial, peripheral place. David writes that 'of all artists ever James Joyce was the most dependent on the particular, on place, site, locality. His lifelong exile served only to sharpen, clarify and deepen his devotion to the *numina* of place, not of any place, but of this place, Eblana . . . *Hircus Civis Eblanensis*, his natal place. Never, perhaps, has such absorption with a microcosm been the means of showing forth the macrocosmic realities. He is the most incarnational of artists.'[11] David concludes his review by stressing Joyce's achievement and the two things which they each had in common: a belief in Thomist aesthetics and an adherence to the Celtic tradition. 'As artist, he was orientated, as fixedly as needle to north, on the end to which a work of art should proceed, namely: wholeness, harmony, radiance. And in some passages the perfection of the art, as such, does preeminently evoke those very qualities. No one, unless by prejudice, could I think deny this, after listening to the fragment from *Anna Livia* on the record issued over twenty years ago by the committee of the Orthological Institute. They did us a great service in making that record, for, like any *bàrd*, Joyce has to be heard to be believed. In this he was indeed of the Celtic tradition.'[12]

In a review of a volume of essays entitled *The Heritage of Early Britain* David offers some explanation of what for him is meant by the Celtic, a concept that was always of vital importance to him. He sees as sentimental the view that the 'Celtic Christian *Weltanschauung* was kindly, tolerant, freedom-loving and romantic'.[13] Rather, he maintains:

There is in the whole Celtic thing an elusive hardness, a bent towards the intricate and towards the abstract, there is also a certain punctiliousness, especially with regard to received formulae. At least some of these same characteristics are, I think, quite clearly observable from La Tène to *Finnegans Wake*. It is easy to miss these qualities in thinking of the early Celtic Christian religious movement because it is next to impossible for us not to feel 'romantic' *about it*. This is so not only because of the particular spirituality of 'the athletes of God', their marvel – voyages and the whole feeling of that springtime and time of nuptials when the Word was made Celtic, but also because of the magical setting of that marriage: the mistcd *insulae*, the white enclosures, the transparencies of water . . . Moreover, that spellbound world is familiar to us, it is the 'demi-paradise' of our own western fringes. Thirdly, the *trouvères* from the beginning utilized that same setting in their mediaeval romance-cycles and Morgana's spell mingles with the spell of sanctity. St. David is Arthur's nephew in one tradition. While it is not necessary to break this spell, it is also necessary when considering the actualities of Celtic Christianity and the contemporaneous art-forms, not to impute to either qualities of which they were innocent. The present reviewer doubts if the virtue of tolerance can have had much place in the religious temper of that age, and certainly 'romantic' is most misleading if applied to the art-forms.[14]

David turned again to the subject of early post-Roman Britain, a favourite topic of his, in a review, published in December 1948, of a volume containing a sequence of poems about King Arthur by Charles Williams, and a commentary on them supplied by C. S. Lewis. The Arthur stories, David here contends, are 'an *Iliad-Aeneid* of the Celtic-Germano-Latin Christian medieval West'.[15] It is interesting that the author of *The Anathemata* faults Charles Williams for antiquarianism and a lack of 'now-ness' in treating King Arthur. 'I don't doubt but what the characters and situations were linked in Williams's mind with "now": but I do not often feel this "now-ness" in the words and images, or rather, I feel it does not inform and pervade the poems as a whole.'[16] But he goes on to concede, and some reviewers of *The Anathemata* would make the same point, that 'now-ness' is an issue for him also. 'This problem of "now-ness" and "then-ness" is so integral for modern artists of all kinds – but I am thinking particularly of the writing of poetry and painting – that it has to be mentioned however foolishly, inadequately, and inexactly one expresses oneself. It is a problem for which there is no escape'.[17]

In the year 1949, a few months after this review was published, David began work on a series of chalice paintings which would occupy him well into the 1950s. These were paintings of flowers, sometimes in a single glass chalice, sometimes in a group of three chalices. A good example of the latter type is *Flora in Calix-Light*, now at Kettle's Yard, Cambridge. It makes much of contrasting textures – petals, glass, the wood of a window, the metal of a window handle. The picture is painted with great delicacy, perhaps even daintiness. It is very charming. But alough the three glass chalices supply an intimation of the sacramental, the picture does not achieve the numinousness, comparable to the Joycean radiance that David surely intended.

In 1951, a year after this series was completed, David was invited by the Royal Academy to become an Associate – but he declined the offer. Some time earlier, at the time when the-then famous painter of horses, Sir Alfred Munnings, was succeeded by Gerald Kelly as President of the Royal Academy, David wrote about his utter rejection of the Academy and of Academic art, in a letter to Jim Ede he burst out: 'What a lot of balls all that stuff is . . . It *is* a rum world that so-called "academic" painting world.' Then, in a way that was very characteristic of him as a letter-writer, he added some more marginal comments: 'it seems to be fundamentally bogus – a vast misapprehension of the nature of the arts and a thing that has outlived its meaning and use'.[18]

Vastly more gratifying to David in 1951 than the chance to become an Associate of the Royal Academy was his completion of the writing of a work with which he had struggled for many years, *The Anathemata*. It seems appropriate that the book, which has for a central theme 'the matter of Britain', should have been finished in the year of the Festival of Britain. On the first day of October David travelled up to London from Harrow and went to the offices of Faber and Faber in Russell Square to personally deliver the manuscript to T. S. Eliot. The two then went out to lunch together. *The Anathemata* was published twelve months later, in the year of the accession of Queen Elizabeth II.

Introduced by a prose Preface of some thirty-five pages, which seeks to explain the intentions behind this difficult work, *The Anathemata* comprises eight titled sections. The first, 'Rite and Fore-time' begins with the words and the actions of a priest celebrating Mass. In his Preface to the book David observed that, 'In a sense the fragments that compose this book are about, or around and about, matters of all sorts which, by a kind of quasi-free association, are apt to stir in my mind at any time and as often as not "in the time of the Mass".'[19] After the opening images of the Mass in the first section there follows a long, rhetorical and extremely erudite meditation on geology evolving into, and producing, pre-history and history. The focus is primarily on Wales but also on the island of Britain generally, and the insistence is that the anthropological process was informed by divine light.

> And over the submerged dryad-ways
>
>   intensively his ray searches
>
> where the alluvium holds
> the polished neoliths
> and where the long mound inhumes
>
>   his neolithic loves
>
> or the round-barrow keeps
>
>   the calcined bones
>
> of these, his still more modern hallows
>
>   that handled the pitiless bronze.[20]

The second section, entitled 'Middle-Sea and Lear-Sea', begins by dating the coming of Christ by relating it to other events in the history of antiquity, such as the siege of Troy and the founding of Rome. Then follows an evocation of a sea-voyage in ancient times out of the Mediterranean, past Gibraltar and the Iberian Peninsula and Biscay, and ending up near Land's End. The section is a pondering and a wondering about the transmission of the Christianity originating by the Mediterranean (Middle-Sea) and ending up in Britain, washed by the Lear-Sea. René Hague, in his *A Commentary on The Anathemata of David Jones* has seen the shipmaster who undertakes this voyage as 'a symbol of Christ guiding man to his haven. Nevertheless there is no Christification of the man himself.'[21]

The third section with the title 'Angle-Land', shows the voyage continuing in time as well as space. The ship moves eastwards through the English Channel and the Straits of Dover and up to the coast of East Anglia, which at this time has been settled by Saxons. Though history is an important subject in *The Anathemata* David is very cavalier with chronology in his approach to the timeless. And quite explicitly so:

when might that be?
when might that be??

I do not know!
I do not know!!
I do not know what time is at
or whether before or after

was it when –
but when *is* when?[22]

The third section ends with a transition from the North Sea in Saxon times to the North Sea in very recent history. The war between the two nations separated by this stretch of water: Britain and Germany is seen as a war of fratricides. The final allusion is to Balin and Balan, two brothers from Malory's *Morte d'Arthur*, who unwittingly killed each other.

147

The fourth section is entitled 'Redriff', the medieval name for present-day Rotherhithe, the place from which David's mother and his formidable grandfather Ebenezer Bradshaw came. The section begins with the speculation that the master of the Mediterranean vessel might not have sailed up into the North Sea but turned westward into the Thames estuary and berthed in the Port of London. And here he would have encountered the uncompromising rectitude of Eb Bradshaw. We are now in Victorian times. Almost three of the four pages that make up this short, fourth section consist of a highly rhetorical declaration by the figure of David's grandfather who demonstrates his determination to do a proper and good job repairing ships and never to cut corners. Here is a brief sample containing specialized and technical vocabulary such as recurs throughout *The Anath-emata.*

> we scamp no repairs here; no botched Riga
> deal nor wood that's all American, softs nor hards, hewn or
> sawn, heart n'r sap, cis- or trans- Gangem-land teak, or fair-
> grained *ulmus* from sylvan wester lands or goodish East Mark
> oak via Fiume in British bottoms
>   let alone
> heart of island-grown
>   seasoned in m'neighbour's yard
> leaves this bench.[23]

'The Lady of the Pool' the fifth section, is the longest in the book. Its title refers to a Cockney lavender-seller who accosts and speaks at length to the Mediterranean skipper when he comes ashore in London. In a letter quoted by René Hague in his *Commentary*, David stated: 'The Lady of the Pool section moves back in time. In "Redriff" we were in the nineteenth century. But the time setting of "The

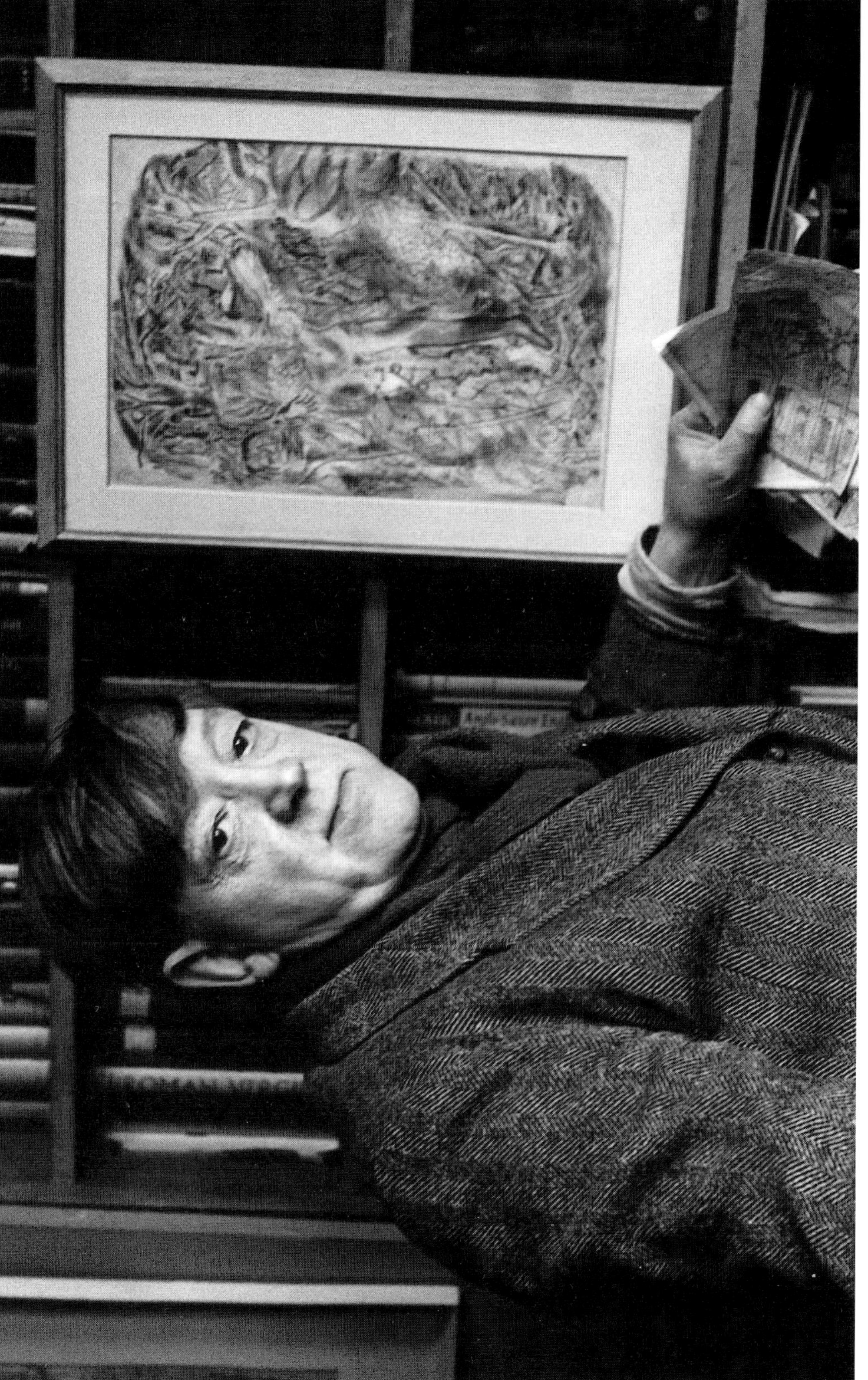

David Jones with the frontispiece of *In Parenthesis*

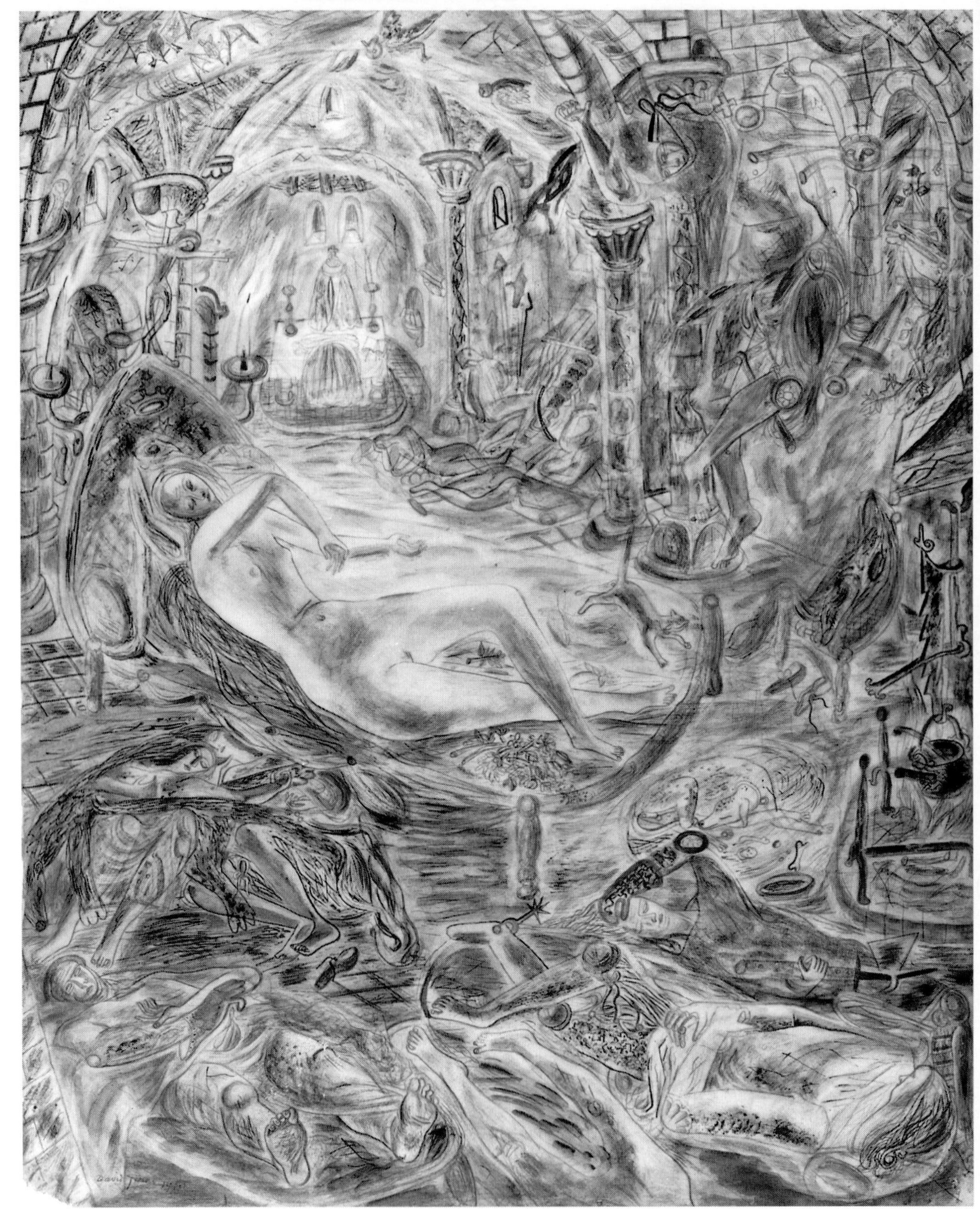

Guenever

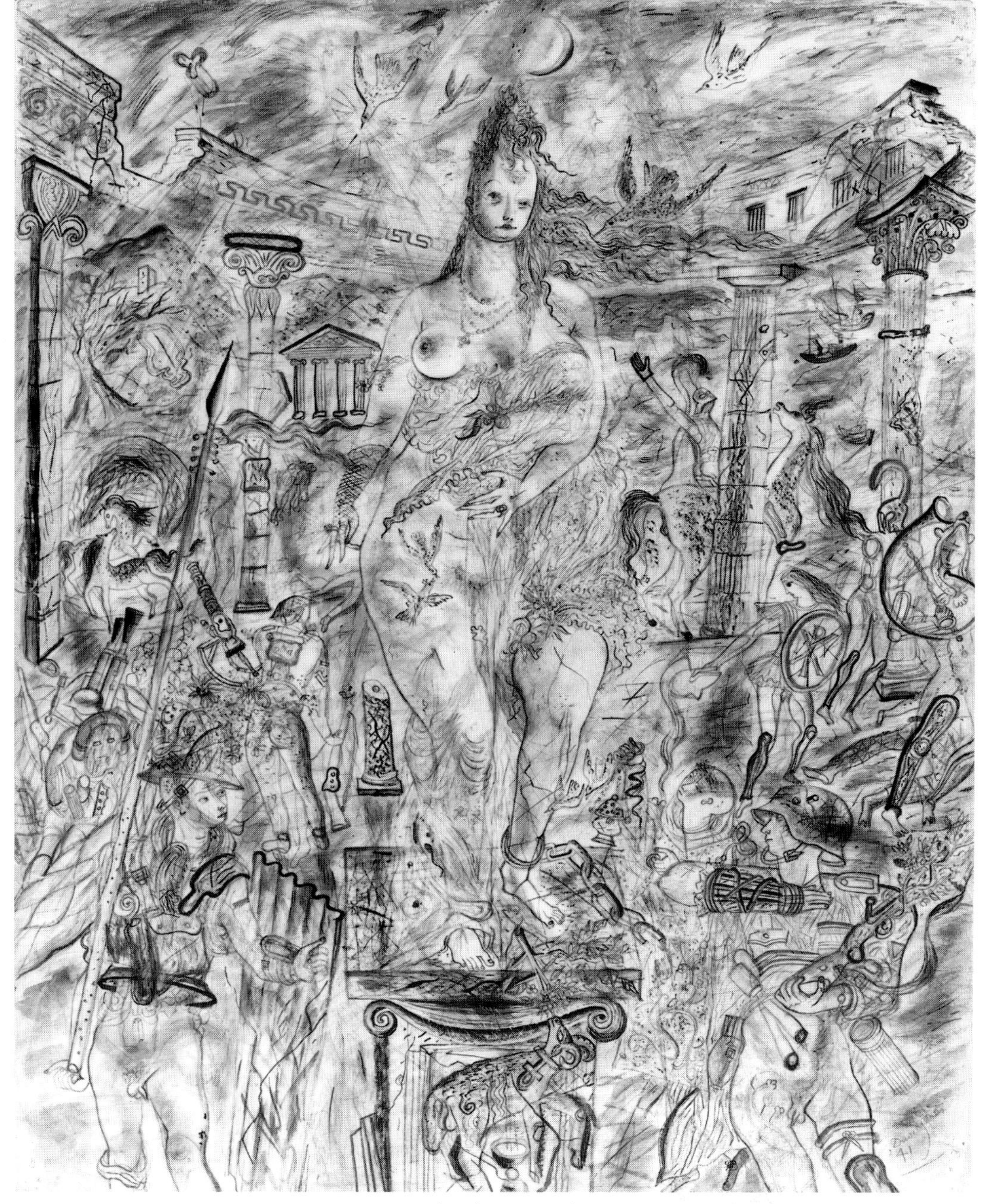

Aphrodite in Aulis

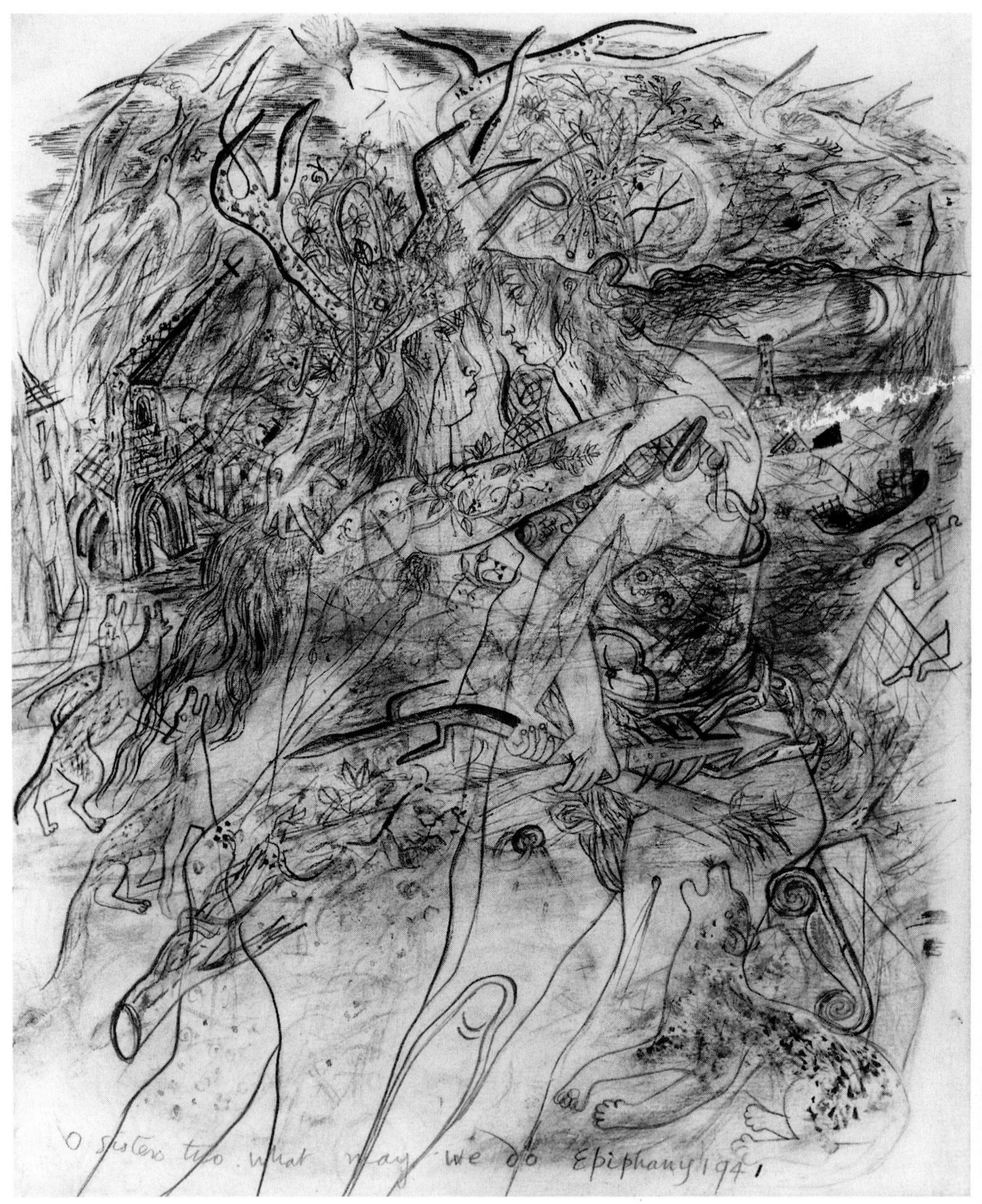

Epiphany 1941: Britannia and Germania Embracing

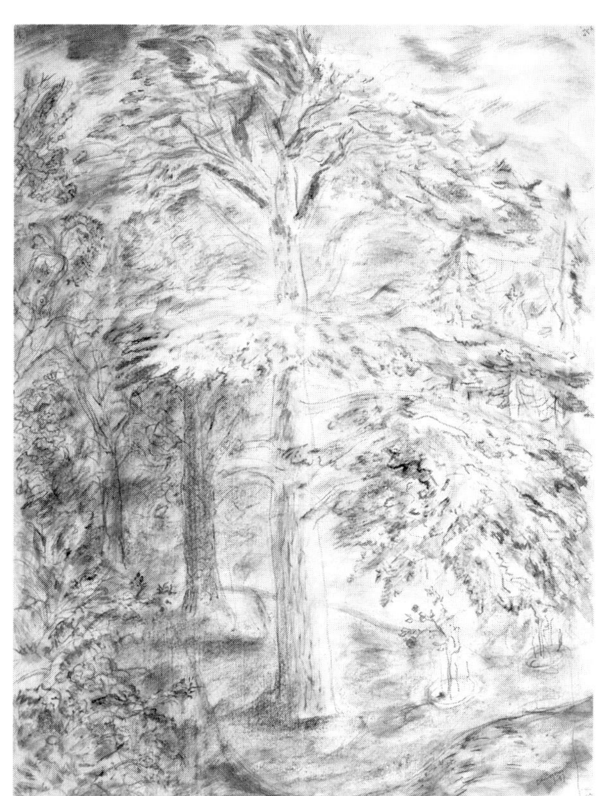

Trees at Bowden House

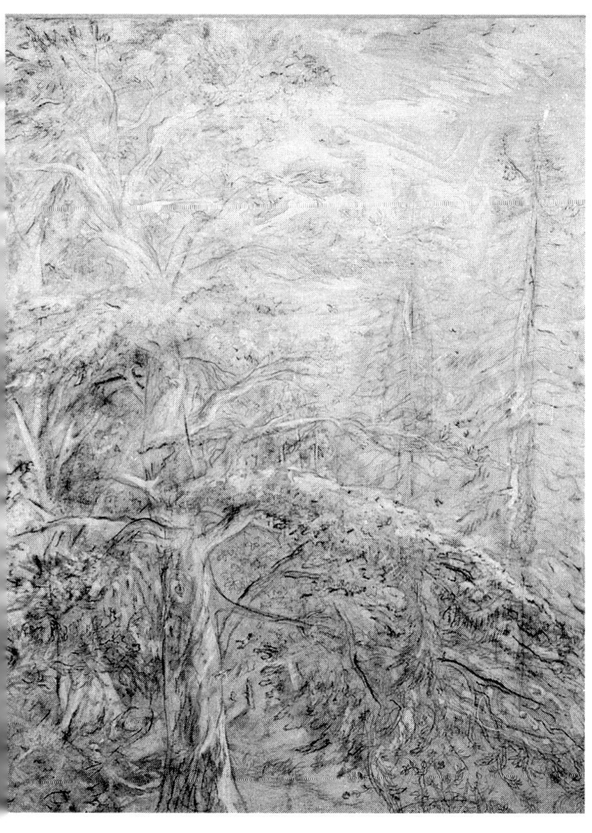

Tys Elvenland

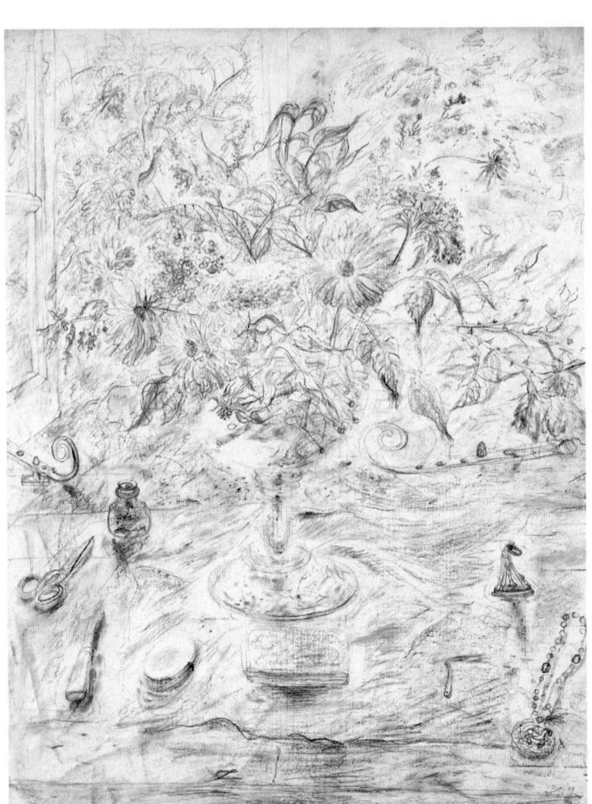

Flowers in a Glass Chalice

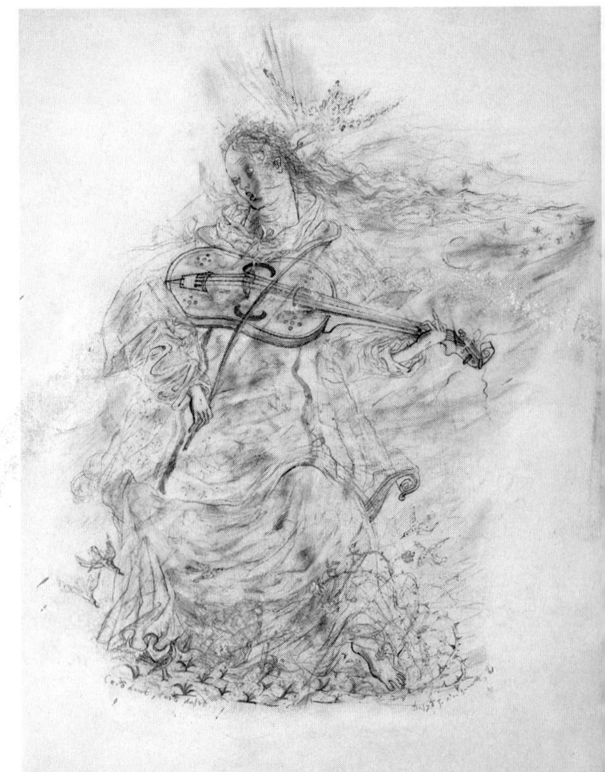

String Song, Tongue Song
– Cerdd Dant, Cerdd Dafod

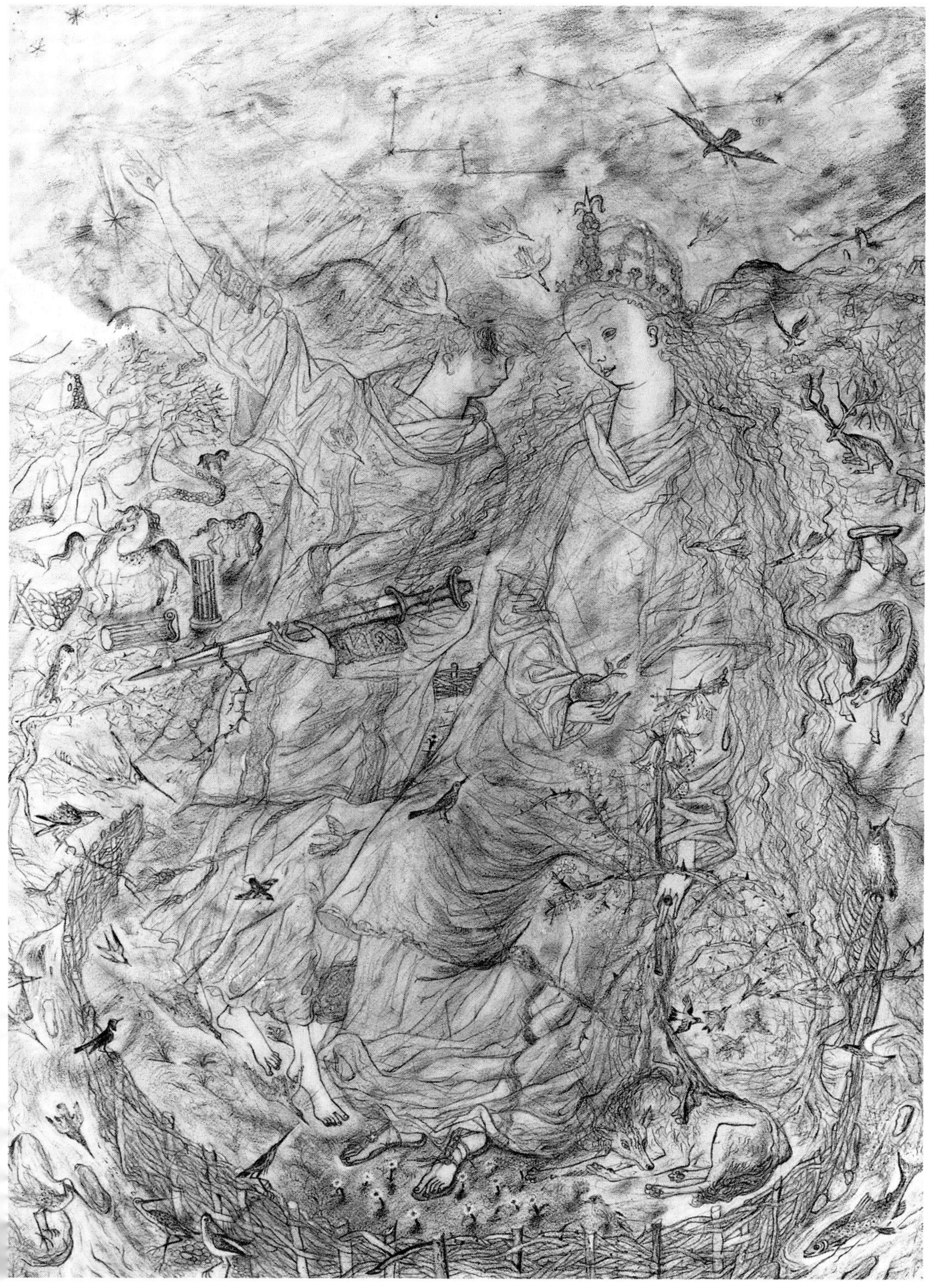

Trystan ac Essyllt

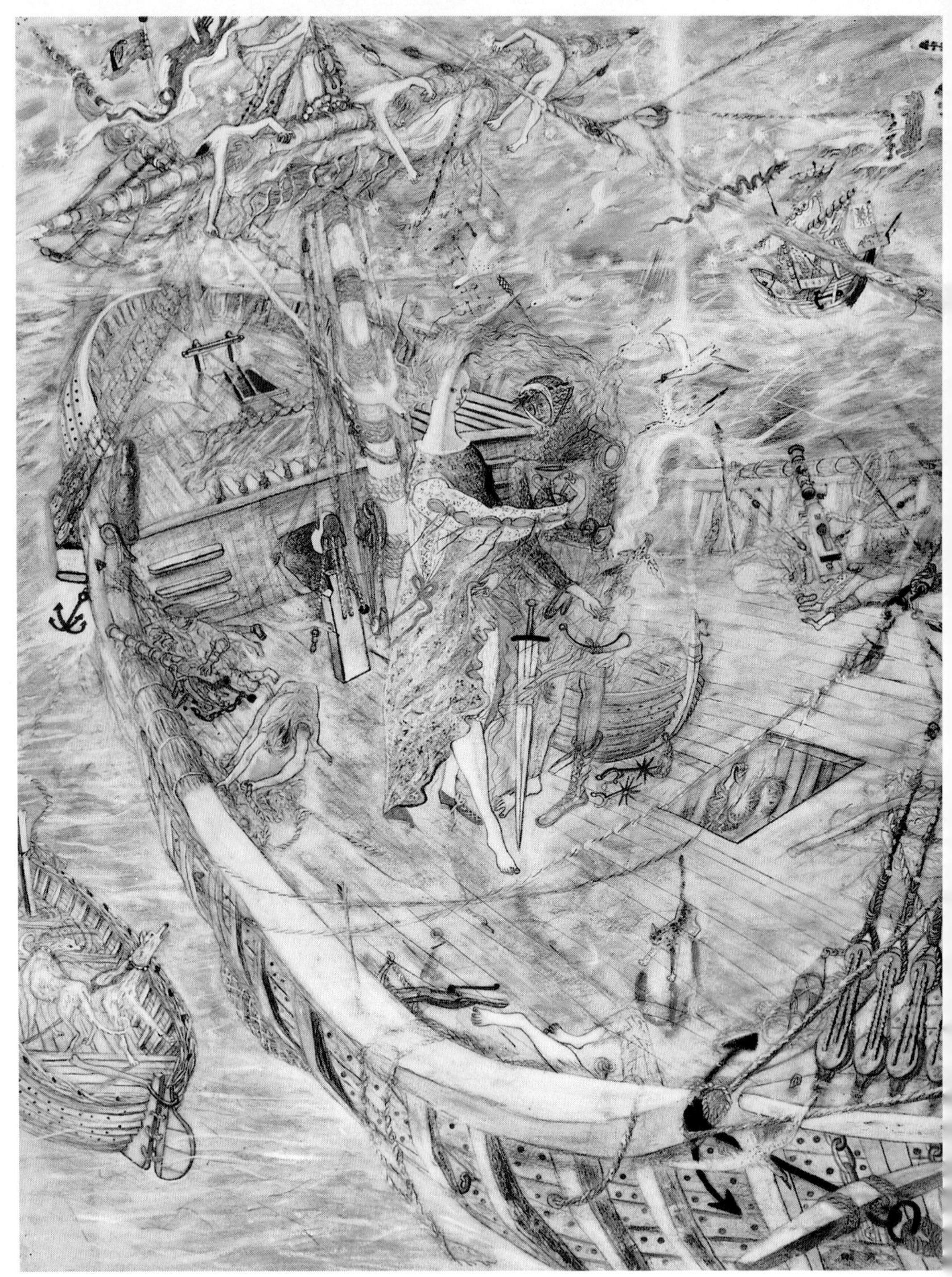

Y Cyfarchiad I Fair (The Greeting to Mary)

Lady in the Pool" is toward the end of the middle ages. There were a number of reasons necessitating this. For one thing she (The Lady of the Pool) had to represent to some extent the British sea thing which rose only after the end of the fifteenth century, so that the figure had to combine the Hogarthian, Turneresque even Dickensian worlds with the Catholic world of "Dick Whittington", Chaucer, Langland, Geoffrey of Monmouth's Trojan – London myth and so on and so on.'[24]

The lavender-seller begins by giving the visiting skipper an evocative listing, sometimes in Cockney rhyming slang, of the many churches in the City of London. Then she tells of her various lovers: there was the young clerk and the mason and various seamen, from all of whom she has learned a great deal. She refers to herself as Britannia and tells of seafaring adventures involving Phoenicians, Egyptians and Saxons. Finally we return to London and to legends surrounding its foundation. She bids goodbye to the captain, whom she calls one of 'you macaroni admirals', and returns to her trade with her street-cry:

> Who'll have
>
> m'living flower?
> Who'll buy my sweet lavender?[25]

Section VI 'Keel, Ram, Stauros' (the last word meaning 'mast') begins with a sequence of speculations about the visiting skipper's activities in London:

> Did he walk the water-lanes of the city from east of Bridge
> Within, by Dowgate and Vintry to Farringdon Without.
> Walking the nine river-fronting divisions of the city
> of cities all, *per se*

> and flower of towns
>   did he hear them say
>   when will you pay me?
>   (or had they not yet grown rich?)[26]

As the skipper returns to his ship the poet thinks of the keel beneath, metaphorizing this length of timber as the Cross of Christ:

> Down
>   far under him
>   the central *arbor*
>   the quivering elm on which our salvation sways.
>   *Baum*, baulk
>   ridging the straked, dark
>   inverted vaults of her.[27]

The poet then considers other applications of the tree, the item in nature that was so central to Christian salvation, and finds it was also used destructively. He describes how over the centuries it evolved as a battering ram. The finale of this section portrays the tree once more as 'vertical'd' and as a creative rather than a destructive instrument: it is the mast of the ship of salvation; it is the Holy Cross, the feast of which is known as Crouchmass.

The seventh section, 'Mabinog's Liturgy', begins by returning to the dating of the Incarnation by placing it in relationship with other historical events. It then proceeds to contemplate certain women: Helen of Troy, Guinevere and, more impressive than either of them, the Virgin Mary. We return to Christ's birth and the elements of the Mass which commemorate it.

The final section, 'Sherthursdaye and Venus Day', focuses on Christ and evokes the Last Supper and the instituting of the Mass on Sherthursdaye, the day before Good Friday and the Crucifixion. The latter part of the section has at its centre the agony of Christ as it is sung in the Good Friday Mass, culminating in the single, painfully, tormented cry 'SITIO' (I thirst).

His cry

from the axile stipe

      at the dry node-height

when the dark cloud brights the trembling lime-rock.

(All known clouds distil showers.

Is there no water in that dark cloud

      for the parched lime-face?

What unknown cloud then, is this?)

As the bleat of the spent stag

      toward the river-course

he, the *fons*-head

      pleading, *ad fontes*

his desiderate cry:

      SITIO[28]

The Anathemata ends, as it began, with reference to the priest celebrating the Mass and to the Christ who created it.

He does what is done in many places

what he does other

      he does after the mode

of what has always been done.

What did he do other

      recumbent at the garnished supper?

What did he do yet other

      riding the Axile Tree?[29]

151

The 1972 paperback edition of *The Anathemata* bears a comment from W. H. Auden that it is 'Very probably the finest long poem written in English this century'. Many critics and scholars writing about David Jones have shared this view, certainly seeing it as his major work. Personally I find *In Parenthesis* the greater poem because of its profound humaneness and of the memorable resonant way in which the humaneness leaves us, as does all great art, with a heightened, more acute sense of our condition. This, however, is not to deny that *The Anathemata* is an impressive piece of writing, albeit a difficult and demanding one. Very occasionally it becomes sentimental, in, for instance the account of the night of the Nativity in 'Mabinog's Liturgy'. But the poem also contains many very beautiful passages. Here, to take just one brief one, is an image of the sea being looked down into at sunset from the deck of a ship.

And suddenly:
        the build of us
        patterns dark the blueing waters
and shadow-gulls
perch the shadows of the yards across the starboard bow-wave
and on the quiet beam water.
           For his chariot
has crossed our course and he stands over Argolis, southward
and westing ane darts back his tangent ray.[30]

Such passages abound, but the work as a whole is more abstract than *In Parenthesis*. The few human characters that appear are very much archetypes burdened with symbolic significance. *The Anathemata* is a work of meditation and frequently of argument and rhetoric, at times of a virtuoso kind. Above all, it is a testimony to David's intense and highly educated Christian faith.

13

Years of Honour
1953–64

IN 1953, THE YEAR of the Queen's Coronation, *The Anathemata* was broadcast on BBC radio and David was impressed by the way Dylan Thomas read some sections of the work. David was also greatly moved by the Coronation of Queen Elizabeth II; it clearly appealed to his feeling for rite and ritual. He recorded a talk for the Welsh Home Service of the BBC entitled 'Wales and the Crown', which was broadcast on 23 July of that year. His argument was that before there was an English or a British Crown there was a Welsh political culture and tradition reaching back into Roman times and beyond. He concluded that:

It is very proper and necessary that the people of Wales should see the monarchy through the eyes of that most complex and unique tradition. It is their special inheritance and it is theirs alone to offer. It is an assortment of gifts in one, small, home-made basket. The poet Martial spoke of a *bascauda* (which word probably means a carrier or basket) that was made in Britain. And our basket, in which we carry these tokens and offerings, is plaited entirely of British wickers. But in that basket are things of very mixed derivation: things Christian and Roman together with things representative of the fragmented tradition of the Brythonic Celts and of their non-Celtic predecessors concerning what the bards have called The White Island, The Honey Isle, the Island of the Mighty and of all that pertains to Britannia the Mother.

For remember there is the tradition of matriarchy, a thing of pre-Celtic provenance working up through the Aryan patriarchy. And, in Wales, Y Mamau the mothers, have always been influential, whether as mortal women or as fairies reflecting the cult of the Deae Matres of Antiquity.[1]

David also riposted strongly to a Catholic contributor to *The Tablet* who maintained that few theologians would allow the word 'sacramental' to be used of 'the present English Coronation rite'.[2] In his letter to the editor of the periodical, he asks 'is it implied that the word would be allowed of the rite used previous to the Reformation?' It seems very probable that David watched the Coronation on television, for he goes on to write about the impression made upon him 'by the actual sight of those rites. What emerged with surprising vividness was the dedicated and sacred figure of immemorial tradition. The impression of regal splendour, let alone of mere pomp, was altogether eclipsed by something far deeper, more primal and quite ageless. The impression was of something sacrificial. A person appeared to have been "made SACRA".'[3]

The Redfern Gallery held a 'Coronation Exhibition' in 1953 and some of David's paintings and drawings were included, although this turned out to be the end of David's long association with the Redfern. In a letter to Rex Nan Kivell, the director of the Gallery, David tells of his anger and distress at the way his paintings had been displayed, and sometimes sold before he had sanctioned their sale. Throughout his life he had a reluctance to part with his work.

Without a commercial dealer, however, his sales dwindled. And so the award in 1954 of a Civil List Pension of £150 per annum was very welcome. As the 1950s proceeded David received increasing recognition from government organizations. In 1954 also, the Welsh Arts Council organized a major retrospective exhibition of his work, taking it to Aberystwyth, to Cardiff, to Swansea, to Edinburgh and finally to the Tate Gallery in London. In May of the following year David was awarded the Order of the British Empire in the Queen's Birthday Honours. He went to Buckingham Palace. When asked by the Queen what he did, he replied that he painted pictures and that Her Majesty's mother, the Queen Mother, had quite a collection of them.

In April of that same year, 1955 David had been invited by the Welsh poet Vernon Watkins to contribute a poem to an issue of *Poetry* (Chicago), that was intended as a memorial to Dylan Thomas who had died two years earlier. Watkins was helping Henry Rago, the editor of *Poetry*, to enlist contributors and to put the issue together. At first David hesitated, telling Watkins: 'You see I never write separate poems . . . I mean it's awfully hard to take a bit out of the kind of stuff I write and publish it as a separate piece.' But in June he sent to Watkins 'The Wall', which he described as 'part of a long thing to do with some Roman auxiliary soldiers on the wall of Jerusalem (on the night of the Last Supper) – it was part of one of the extensive chunks of material that belonged to *The Anathemata* in one of its various stages'. In July he wrote to tell Watkins that he had received a letter from Henry Rago expressing admiration for the poem and accepting it for publication. 'The Wall' appeared in *Poetry* in November 1955.

There is something historically appropriate in David being published in that particular magazine. *Poetry* had first become important in the history of literature in English when during the First World War its editor Harriet Monroe, of Chicago, appointed Ezra Pound, then resident in London, to be the magazine's foreign editor. In 1915 Pound was responsible for *Poetry* publishing 'The Love Song of J. Alfred Prufrock' by his friend, T. S. Eliot. The Modernist movement in poetry had begun.

'The Wall' continues very much in that poetic tradition. Like parts of Pound's *Cantos* and Eliot's *Four Quartets*, David's poem is in free verse that is sometimes close to prose. The lowly, weary soldier who speaks the dramatic monologue meditates on Rome, its empire and imperialism, though his language is often that of the First World War. The conclusion clearly alludes to the Cold War, which in 1955 was part of the world order:

> but now they say the Quirinal Mars
> turns out to be no god of war but of armed peace.[4]

There is also a metaphor for the consumer society that was establishing itself in the 1950s. This is 'little Plutus, the gold-getter, and they say that sacred brat has a future'. Defending prosperity is the soldier's new duty:

> we shall continue to march
> round and round the cornucopia:
> that's the new fatigue.[5]

The poem was a success. It was awarded the Harriet Monroe Memorial Prize by *Poetry*, was broadcast on the

BBC and in 1957 was published in Britain for the Poetry Book Society in a poetry supplement entitled *Landmarks and Voyages*.

Yet despite all the public recognition he was receiving David's private life was not particularly happy. His health deteriorated during the mid-1950s, he had problems with his eyes and was often enervated with bouts of depression; he often had to report the return of 'Rosie'. Nevertheless he managed to keep working as a poet, an essayist and a painter and some of his most ambitious painted inscriptions belong to these years. He was encouraged in his efforts by the admiration of young men who were drawn to him and to his work. In late 1957 he began corresponding with twenty-six-year-old William Hayward, who was writing a commentary on *The Anathemata*. Hayward, who had been an undergraduate at Merton College, Oxford, and taken a degree in English, was the recipient of some important letters from David about his work, including nearly four pages of corrections to the first edition of *The Anathemata*. In 1979, five years after David's death, *Letters to William Hayward*, edited by Colin Wilcockson, was published by Agenda Editions. The book constitutes an important companion work to the poem. Wilcockson was another of David's young friends. Also from Merton College and the future editor, for Macmillan, of a selection from Langland's *Piers Plowman*, a work greatly admired by David, Wilcockson had met David when he lived at Northwick Park Lodge in the early months of 1955. After Wilcockson's departure the friendship continued with letters and visits until the end of David's life, and they often corresponded about literary subjects. But David would write frequently about his depression and 'a devastating *weariness*' and 'tedious worries'.[6]

Then, in 1958, he had a most exciting and revitalizing

experience. At the age of sixty-two he fell in love again, violently. The last love of his life was Valerie Price, a Welsh woman in her mid-twenties. She was a schoolteacher, an actress, a model, a physiotherapist and, in Wales, a champion hurdler. She was a fervent Welsh nationalist and a member of Plaid Cymru. It was as a result of seeing one of David's letters about Welshness in the correspondence columns of *The Times* that she got in touch with him. He invited her to Northwick Park Lodge and she came to visit him accompanied by her fiancé, Michael Wynne-Williams (who was also Welsh). David and Valerie took to each other immediately. In a letter to a friend David gave a lengthy analysis of the relationship that now developed, saying that it was 'partly physical' but more like a kind of 'dumb compassion – and a *mutual* compassion between two people *wholly remote* from each other in most respects'.[7]

David always used the Welsh form of her first name, Elri, and said in another letter that her Welshness had 'an awful lot to do with my intrication with Elri. She's the only Welsh woman I've ever really met . . .'[8] He became utterly lovesick, phoning and writing to her constantly. On her birthday he sent her an expensive bunch of roses. Elri's attitude to David, on the other hand, was a mixture of respect and kindness. But at one point in the relationship his attentions to her would appear to have become so obsessive that for some months she would not see him. Then she relented and he was overjoyed when she accepted his invitation to lunch at the Paddington Hotel.

In 1959 Elri married Michael Wynne-Williams. For a wedding gift David wrote them a poem that imagined them as a confluence of two Welsh rivers. He presented the poem to them as a painted inscription. Elri must have been charmed by the gift. Nevertheless, after her marriage she distanced herself somewhat from David. But she remained a good and helpful friend, often assisting him in practical matters. She would do his laundry and help him when, with difficulty, he entertained in his single room. William Blissett remembered that she also made arrangements for his framed pictures, portfolios and papers to be stored in the vaults of Coutts' Bank. But for all her practical concern, David was unhappy about the cooling of her involvement with him. In a letter of 1960 he recalled how seeing Elri made him feel 'quite young again'. But, he went on, 'now I feel useless and aged . . .'

But disappointed and saddened as he was in his private life, public honours continued to come to him. In 1959, with his finances as precarious as ever, he had been persuaded by a friend to apply for an award from the Bollingen Foundation in America. His application was supported by Herbert Read, W. H. Auden, Stephen Spender, Kathleen Raine, Christopher Dawson, Father Martin D'Arcy, Kenneth Clark and T. S. Eliot. He had to fill in what he called a 'yard-long' questionnaire which, coming as it did from 1950s America, required him to say, among other things, that he was not, nor ever had been a member of the Communist Party. In answer to the question: 'What are the aims and purposes of your work' he supplied a very clear and succinct piece of self-definition:

I am in no sense a scholar, but an artist, and it is paramount for any artist that he should use whatever happens to be to hand. For artists depend on the immediate and the contractual and their apperception must have a 'now-ness' about it. *But*, in our present megalopolitan technocracy the artist must still remain a 'rememberer' (part of the official bardic function in earlier phases of society). But in the totally changed and rapidly changing circumstances of today this ancient function takes on a particular significance. For now the artist becomes, willy-nilly, a sort of Boethius, who has been nick-named 'the Bridge', because he carried forward into an altogether metamorphosed world certain of the fading oracles which had sustained antiquity. My view is that all artists, whether they know it or not, whether they would repudiate the notion or not, are in fact 'showers forth' of things which tend to be impoverished, or misconceived, or altogether lost or wilfully set aside in the preoccupations of our present intense technological phase, but which nonetheless belong to man.

So when asked to what end does my work proceed I can do no more than answer in the most tentative and hesitant fashion imaginable, thus: Perhaps it is in the maintenance of some sort of single plank in some sort of bridge.[9]

His Bollingen application was successful. But trouble followed. The British Inland Revenue learned about his grant and insisted that it be taxed. David protested strongly because he knew that other British recipients of such awards had not been taxed. When the Inland Revenue proved to be inflexible David took the matter to court. Letters in support of his case from Herbert Read and T. S. Eliot were disallowed by the judge. The precedent on which the case turned was a judgment concerning a gift from Lord Bute to a winning jockey. The ludicrousness of this made David laugh, and laugh loudly. He was sternly called to order by the court. Unfortunately the judgment finally went against him and he had to pay the tax.

But still recognition continued to come his way. The year after his volume of essays *Epoch and Artist* was published in 1959, it won an award of £100 from the Welsh Arts Council. Also in 1960 David was made an honorary Doctor of Literature by the University of Wales. In 1961 he became a Fellow of the Royal Society of Literature and also a member of the Royal Watercolour Society. The following year he received an award of £200 from the Society of Authors Travelling Fund.

In 1961 he was published again in *Poetry* of Chicago. This time the poem was 'The Tutelar of the Place', which Vernon Watkins, by now a close friend, had helped him to edit and had typed out for him. The guardian referred to in the title is the creative female principal who appears to mankind in various guises, including of course that of the Virgin Mary. For David she is both one and many. She has different names in different places:

> wherever in which of the wide world-ridings
> you must not call her but by that name
> which accords to the morphology of that place.[10]

Early in the poem man's relationship with the goddess is metaphorized as that of a young boy and his sister quietly and unselfconsciously playing together. (The passage surely derives from David's memories of happy times spent with his sister Alice in childhood.) The second half of the poem is a prayer to the goddess for protection against the standardization enforced by the imperialisms in the history of the world.

> Queen of the differentiated sites, administratix of the demarcations, let our cry come unto you.
> In all times of imperium save us when the
> *mercatores* come save us . . .[11]

The writing in the poem is impressive. The word 'pied' in the following passage in the prayer clearly serves to recall Gerard Manley Hopkins, and the comparison is one which 'The Tutelar of the Place' can sustain.

> mother of particular perfections
> queen of otherness
> mistress of asymmetry
> patroness of things counter, parti, pied, several
> protectress of things known and handled
> help of things familiar and small
> wardress of the secret crevices
> of things wrapped and hidden
> mediatrix of all the deposits
> margravine of the troia
> empress of the labyrinth
> receive our prayers.[12]

The early 1960s was also a good period for David as a painter as well as a poet. He completed two major paintings, one of which – a fine work of 1963 – is *Y Cyfarchiad I Fair* or *The Greeting to Mary*, now in the National Museum of Wales. The painting shows the crowned Virgin as a young Welsh woman seated in a wattled bower. The surrounding landscape is reminiscent of that around Capel-y-ffin and is full of birds and animals. Mary's visitant points dramatically upwards with his right arm, his facial expression intense, insistent, even peremptory. The poignancy of the work centres on the expression of the Virgin, as gently, submissively, in a trancelike way she ponders the many implications of his annunciation to her. Some of these are intimated by the large sword he carries, by the thorns that are attached to it and by the broken column in the middle distance. There are lines that link and emphasize the stars in the two constellations in the sky behind Mary and Gabriel. These are the constellations of Virgo and Libra, the former associated by David with the Cross. He once noted that 'according to the Fourth Gospel there stood, next to the Cross, the Mother'.

A far different image of womanhood dominates the other important picture that David also completed in 1963. This is *Trystan ac Essylt* (or 'Tristan and Isolde' in more familiar spelling), a painting on which he worked for three years or so, often in a state of great frustration with it. At one point he felt that he could not go on with it, telling René Hague that he felt 'quite exhausted by the complications'. Though certainly a very intricate work, the central image and subject are simple enough. Of the two famous lovers Iseult is shown here to be by far the more forceful. Her tall figure and her brightly coloured dress are the centre of the picture space. Tristan, standing retiringly behind her, is but a drab brown ghost and takes up far less room. Iseult may look doll-like, but she steps forward strongly, confidently. She is the assertive, purposeful female. She is also, of course, a destructive one. David here returns again to his contemplation of sexual love as a destroyer. But in this painting he contextualizes the subject in an exceptionally complex way. The heavens above the lovers, the sea and the ship, are all richly endowed with relevant iconographic detail and implication. It is a painting to linger long upon and to ponder, for it is by far the most elaborate, referentially, of his paintings. Whilst working on it he told Janet Stone that 'before I can deal with Tristan and his girl on the main deck of my windswept ship I've got to find out all manner of stuff in some detail – not for accuracy's sake at all – for that doesn't matter a damn – but in order to get the feel of the thing . . .'[13]

Trystan ac Essyllt was the last picture that David was

able to complete. He would occasionally paint inscriptions for friends in his last years, but broadly speaking this work marks the end of his career as a painter. For in 1962, as he moved towards finishing it, his illness struck again. By 1963 he was once more in a state of breakdown. On this occasion, Dr Bill Stevenson and his colleagues had to conclude that their earlier mode of treatment no longer worked. They decided to resort to drugs to alleviate his condition. He was prescribed Nardil to mitigate his rapidly intensifying agoraphobia, but this medication did nothing for his insomnia and memory loss. He was also given the powerful tranquillizer Nembutal, as well as Trofanil phenobarbitone, Drinaryl and Librium. There was such a large number of drugs for him to take during the day that he felt it necessary to make a coloured timetable to remind him, and even then he sometimes got it wrong. After several months of this treatment he did not feel much better but was painfully aware that his drug-induced confusion and drowsiness were preventing him from working.

But he did have some good days and some happy experiences. One memorable occasion for him was in May 1963 when Stephen Spender brought the eighty-one-year-old Russian composer Igor Stravinsky, who was a great admirer of David's work, to Harrow to see him. Stravinsky was accompanied by his wife, and Spender brought his wife, Natasha, who was also a musician. Despite the number of people present in David's cluttered room it was an extremely happy visit. At first David was somewhat in awe of the composer of *Petrushka* and *Le Sacre du Printemps* because, perhaps surprisingly for one who greatly emphasized the role and significance of sound in his poetry, his musical tastes and knowledge were somewhat limited. Prudence Pelham had once remarked that he ruled out 'anything after 14th. Cent. Except of course

164

Negro Spirituals and "Frankie and Johnny were Lovers" and "Casey Jones Mounted on his Engine" and "Six Dukes Went a Fishing".'[14] And David himself told a correspondent that he did not 'get much beyond plainsong and early polyphony and folk – and primitive music'.[15] One record which he especially prized was of a canzone by Guillaume Dufay, which was a setting of words by Petrarch. Very likely he talked about this with his guests; certainly he was very interested to learn from Stravinsky that the Pope was a considerable musicologist and a scholar. During the time Stravinsky had lived in Venice he had met the Pope who was Cardinal there at that time. He was much impressed by the large-scale work which the future pope had written on the sixteenth century saint, cardinal and theologian, Charles Borromeo.

Stephen Spender noticed that David had 'under his bed a very old gramophone of the kind that winds up with a handle'. He also remembered David playing on it 'a worn record of plain-song Gregorian chant, almost inaudible to us through the rasp of the steel needle, while with hands clasped across his knees and an expression of bliss on his face, he swayed to and fro to the imagined music.'[16] Before the guests departed David spread out some of his paintings and drawings for them to see, beginning with *The Lion*, which he had drawn as a child. As the Spenders and the Stravinskys set off back to London the Russian composer remarked that visiting David was 'like visiting a holy man in his cell'.[17]

But other visitors were more uncomfortable. They were perturbed by David's illness and the effects of his medication. His friends and acquaintances were worried about his often dazed state. T. S. Eliot was particularly concerned. He and David had continued to be friendly after the publication of *The Anathemata*, and Eliot had got Faber to commission David to illustrate 'The Cultivation of Christmas Trees', the poem Eliot contributed to Fabers' series of little booklets entitled *Ariel Poems*. (The drawing is an allusion to the stag in the Wilton Diptych, that David had contemplated many years before as an art student with his teacher A. S. Hartrick.) Eliot, who was interested in the poetry that David was still struggling to write, knew a great deal about the effect of drugs, for they had had a devastating effect on his first wife Vivien, who had spent the last years of her life confined in a mental institution. Eliot gently remonstrated with David and also got Harman Grisewood to speak to him on this subject – but to no avail. David was by now becoming habituated to his treatment and was convinced that without Nembutal he would not sleep.

In March 1964 he published 'The Dream of Private Clitus' in the first number of the magazine *Art and Literature*. It is eight pages long, the first seven being in prose and the last in free verse. It relates how a Roman soldier, serving on the German front, had a dream in which he saw an image of the Tellus Mater, the Earth Mother, reach down to him. The image, the marble relief of the Tellus Mater, is on the east front of the Ara Pacis Augustae, facing the Flaminian Way leading north out of Rome. At precisely that moment of dream-vision his Celtic comrade Lugobelinos cries out 'Modron', and the Roman Clitus concludes that 'his Modron and our Matrona are one'. The two different parts of the Empire see the same female deity under different names and forms, but such dreams and visions, the last page tells us, are denied to a 'fact-man' such as Brasso, an officer interested only in power and advancement. The piece repeats some of the notions present in 'The Tutelar of the Place' but is more schematic and tendentious. It is the least successful of the Roman fragments and the diminished quality of David's writing here may well have been caused by his poor state of health.

In 1964, the second year of his treatment, David sustained a major blow. There came the news that year that Northwick Park Lodge was to be closed. The prospect of moving terrified him; his fragile consititution could not tolerate change. He clung to his 'dug-out' and refused to leave until finally friends persuaded him to accept the inevitable. They found him a room at the Monksdene Residential Hotel and he agreed to go.

But nevertheless the move in April 1964 was saddening and difficult. To a friend he wrote, 'with some suddenness the house is being closed down and I'm in the chaos of trying to deal with 14 years accumulation of stuff in this one beloved room'. As David tried to settle into the new, unfamiliar surroundings, he told the same correspondent: 'I sadly miss being up at Northwick Lodge, in my high room, but the house closed down, and, now it has been pulled down so you would not know it had ever been there.'[18]

Monksdene Residential Hotel was at 2 Northwick Park in Harrow, at the foot of the Hill and very much in suburban Metroland. It was a large Victorian house that had been converted and it was rather shabby. Michael Alexander remembered that the walls of the cramped entrance hall had the 'heavy red-and-gold embossed wallpaper that used to be universal in the Indian restaurants.'[19] Another visitor thought that the hotel's curly wrought ironwork made it look like 'a Moroccan brothel'. David's room on the ground floor was oblong and rather dark, about fifteen feet by twelve, and one or two of his watercolours had been hung on the walls. Michael Alexander noted that David's bed was piled so high with books and papers, all so disordered, that it was hard to believe that it was ever slept in. Otherwise the facilities consisted of a gas ring and a kettle. His meals were brought to him on a tray.

Through French windows in his room he could look out onto a garden, though soon after his arrival the garden was destroyed and the space made into a car park. In this brutal setting David struggled to work, when his health allowed, on several related poems about the Romans in the Holy Land. One of these poems, 'The Fatigue', published about eighteen months after his move, views the Crucifixion through the eyes of the soldiers ordered to carry it out. They speak the language of British Tommies of the First World War. In this way the climactic story in Christ's life is made contemporary and realistic to modern readers. But the poem has its visionary language too, for the soldiers are:

> those who handle the instruments
> who *are* the instruments
> to hang the gleaming Trophy
> on the Dreaming Tree[20]

'The Fatigue' was printed at Rampant Lions Press in Cambridge a year after David's removal to Monksdene Residential Hotel. Will Carter and his son Sebastian, who ran this small press, published the work 'as a token of affection and esteem from friends and admirers of David Jones on the occasion of his seventieth birthday, November 1st. 1965'. Will Carter, a renowned printer, typographer and letter-cutter, had been approached in 1963 by Douglas Cleverdon to print an edition of *The Rime of the Ancient Mariner* with ten copper engravings done by David in 1928. In 1981, seven years after David's death, the Carters, under the imprint Clover Hill, produced the sumptuous *Engravings of David Jones*.

14

The Last Decade
1964–74

THERE WERE SOME CONSOLATIONS for David in
1964, the year of his enforced departure from
Northwick Park Lodge. He was awarded the Gold
Medal at the Royal National Eisteddfod. But his agoraphobia now had such a grip on him that he was unable to
travel to Wales to attend the presentation ceremony. However, he was greatly pleased to receive the Eisteddfod
catalogue and to read what his friend, the Welsh poet
Vernon Watkins, had written about him in it. 'Wales is
today honouring an artist who has already honoured her,'
declared Watkins, concluding with a very apt and succinct
characterization of David's work as 'a religious vision
projecting a symbolic art, and through this art, whether
in literature, painting or drawing, shines his love of man
and of all that is precious to him, and a particular love of
Wales and these islands drawn from the roots of earliest
customs and ways of living'.[1]

Around this time David was also very gratified to see his
work assessed thoughtfully and admiringly in a place he
would not have expected, the *New Yorker*. In its issue of 22
August there was an extended review by Harold Rosenberg

169

of *Epoch and Artist*, David's volume of essays. David called the review 'The only proper criticism of that heterogeneous collection of stuff that's ever appeared since it came out here in 1959. Mr. Rosenberg had really got down to what either implicitly or explicitly runs through the whole.'[2]

Another pleasure for David in the summer of 1964 was his attendance at the first communion of Rebecca Rose Fraser, daughter of the prominent Catholic Sir Hugh Fraser, then head of the House of Fraser, and of his wife, the writer Lady Antonia Fraser. Rebecca Rose was David's god-daughter. For the occasion he painted an inscription, which he gave her when he went to the celebration lunch at the family's home in Campden Hill Square. He was much entertained by, and in sympathy with, Sir Hugh's jokes about the vernacularization of the Roman Catholic Mass. The loss of the Latin liturgy never ceased to appal David.

Around this time he also met one of his fellow world war one writers, Siegfried Sassoon. David found him 'extremely nice, gentle and pleasant'.[3] The two men were brought together by Alan Lascelles who worked at Court. They talked about 'details of trench life at various times and in various sectors', and about Robert Graves's *Good-bye to All That*.[4]

On 29 October there was the fiftieth anniversary dinner of the London Welsh Battalion of the Royal Welch Fusiliers. David was invited and very much wanted to go, but he couldn't. His state of health was such that he simply could not face a trip to London. How bad his agoraphobia could be was demonstrated when a friend, the painter Sarah Balme, arranged to take him to London in 1966 to see the Bonnard exhibition at the Royal Academy. It was to be a treat for him because Pierre Bonnard was one of his favourite artists and a major influence on his own painting, particularly his interiors and his very appealing window paintings. Some six years earlier, in 1960, David had written to a friend, saying that he wished that 'there were more Bonnards in England – he's a chap I'm very fond of. I think he's the best of those marvellous French painters of that period. More magical than Degas by far. He seemed to be able to suck out "poetry" from just about everything.'[5]

Fortunately, in 1966, a large number of Bonnards had been brought to London and Sarah Balme and David drove with great anticipation from Harrow to Piccadilly to see them. Sarah dropped David off in the forecourt of the Royal Academy where he was to wait for her while she drove away to park the car. But the moment she left him David was seized by a terrifying panic, and when Sarah returned he was in an agony of fright. She sat him down and was finally able to calm him. When he had fully recovered they were able to go into the gallery to look at the Bonnard paintings which delighted them both. *Nue à la Baignoire* and other paintings of Bonnard's wife Marthe in the bath particularly appealed to David.

In the spring of 1965 David published a new poem, 'The Hunt', which appeared in *Agenda*. Some four and a half pages long, partly prose and partly lineated free verse, it is clearly a fragment from a larger work. Dealing with an episode in the life of King Arthur it has close affiliations with *The Sleeping Lord*. In a note David explained that 'The Hunt' was 'based on the native Welsh early medieval prose-tale, Culhwch ac Olwen, in which the predominant theme becomes the great hunt across the whole of southern Wales of the boar Trwyth by all the war-bands of the Island led by Arthur.'[6]

Though David was frequently ill during the course of writing 'The Hunt', the piece shows that as a writer he was still capable of a great verbal richness and power. Here is part of the description of King Arthur charging through the forest after the boar, often wounding himself as he forces his way through the thickets:

> If his embroidered habit is clearly from a palace wardrobe it is mired and rent and his bruised limbs gleam from between the rents, by reason of the excessive fury of his riding when he rode the close thicket as though it were an open launde
>
>   (indeed, was it he riding the forest-ride or was the tangled forest riding?)
>
> for the thorns and flowers of the forest and the bright elm -shoots and the twisted tanglewood of stamen and stem clung and meshed him and starred him with variety
>
> and the green tendrils gartered him and briary-loops galloon him with splinter-spike and broken blossom twining his royal needlework
>
>   and ruby petal-points counter the countless points of his wounds.[7]

In the spring of the following year, 1966, David was greatly saddened to learn of the death of his benefactress, Helen Sutherland, on 29 April. Along with the £5,000 which she had bequeathed to him in her will, she also left him in a codicil: 'a chronometer, my scissors, my ivory paper knife, knee rug, shawl and blanket and some tea cups'. Two executors of the will were Nicolete Gray and her husband Basil Gray, Keeper of Oriental Antiquities at the British Museum. To Nicolete Gray Helen Sutherland bequeathed her entire collection of paintings and *objets d'art* which included many paintings by David. In the codicil to her will she asked the executors not to sell her Cumberland home at Cockley Moor but to consider whether 'it could by any means be saved and preserved both on account of its unique situation and character and in order that it might be used for the benefit of scholars, artists (whether musicians, painters, writers or "makers" of any kind) and Religious whether for Retreats of Devotion (I believe a Retreat house is needed in this diocese) or for intellectual, creative or spiritual work . . .'

Helen Sutherland's death was noticed twice in *The Times*. Her obituary published on 2 May 1966 recalled how 'she gave to the artists of her choice, Ben Nicholson, David Jones, Winifred Nicholson, Barbara Hepworth, not only the continuous financial support which made so much difference in those years, but friendship and an appreciation which was extremely sensitive and also ruthless.' The obituarist continued: 'In her own houses, and in the way in which she lived in them, Helen Sutherland created her own art. In Lowndes Square, Rock Hall in Northumberland and Cockley Moor in Matterdale she used the wealth which she had inherited to create the sort of perfection in which she believed.' The obituary ended by stating that 'she made a unity out of her life and all her interests, and at the centre of this was her Christianity, both as a member of the Society of Friends and later as a Catholic Anglican.'

Four days later, on 6 May *The Times* published a further brief article entitled 'Miss Helen Sutherland', contributed by Janet Adam Smith. She began by developing the concluding point made in the obituary: 'Everything in Helen Sutherland's daily life was an act of choice and creation – her clothes, her food and wine, the flowers which "just put in as they are" looked more beautiful than other people's arrangements, the exquisitely-penned letters which perhaps more than anything her friends will miss.' The writer concedes that 'friends sometimes felt that her standards were too exacting, and she could pounce alarmingly on lapses'. Janet Adam Smith's final observation happens to give a good indication of Helen Sutherland's affinity with David. 'For all her concern with works of art, her values were by no means exclusively aesthetic; her delight in painting and sculpture was part of her delight in, and reverence for, the whole created world, one manifestation of her Christianity.'

During the spring and summer of 1966 as he came to terms with the loss of this long-standing friend and patroness, David was making a selection of his drawings to be reproduced in a 'David Jones Special Issue' of *Agenda*. The issue was devoted entirely to his work and contained essays on all aspects of it. *Agenda*, founded and edited by William Cookson was, in the 1960s and later, the place where the best and most important British poetry appeared. The magazine printed new work by, and devoted special issues to such great, but at that time largely unrecognized poets such as Basil Bunting and Hugh MacDiarmid, as well as David Jones. Indeed, it was *Agenda* that helped us to see that these poets constituted a generation of British Modernism subsequent to and deriving from, that of Ezra Pound and T. S. Eliot, who had founded the Modernist movement in the 1910s and 1920s.

The *Agenda* 'David Jones Special Issue' of spring-summer 1967 contained six of his poems, two of them – 'A, a, a, Domine Deus' and 'The Sleeping Lord' – previously unpublished. The former is a thirty-one-line lyric expressing the poet's dismay, even despair, in his failing quest to know God among the synthetic and non-creaturely artefacts that make up the environment of a modern technological civilization:

> I have journeyed among the dead forms
> causation projects from pillar to pylon.
> I have tired the eyes of the mind
>> regarding the colours and lights.
> I have felt for His Wounds
>> in nozzles and containers.[8]

The second new poem in the Special Issue was 'The Sleeping Lord', a very substantial and verbally intricate poem running to some twenty-six pages. It is a visionary contemplation of the figure alluded to in the title who is an amalgam of Christ and King Arthur. In the vision the lordly figure is seen attended by his footholder and his candlebearer. The description of the ceremonial candle is a good example of the delicate verbal particularizations in this poem. The Light-Bearer holds

> the tall, tapering, flax-cored candela of pure wax . . .
> that flames upward
> in perfection of form
> like the leaf-shaped war-heads
> that gleam from the long-halfed spears
> of the lord's body-guard
> but immeasurably greater
> is the pulchritude
> for the quivering gleam of it
> is of living light.[9]

The sleeping lord is also attended by the Priest of the Household who, as he celebrates the Mass, repeatedly 'makes memento' of individuals from the Welsh and British past. The poem is about 'men who loved the things of the Island' and contains numerous evocations of places and landscapes. Most of the places are Welsh and there are many Welsh words and phrases in the work; it is a poem about language and about Welsh and English as comparative languages on this island. However, not all the Welsh places described are beautiful. Here is the evocation of the South Welsh coalfields as the poet using the often excited interrogative approach which runs through the poem to ask about the sleeping lord, and employs the Welsh word for slaves, *caethion*.

> Are his wounded ankles
> > lapped with the ferric waters
> that all through the night
> > hear the song
> from the night-dark seams
> > where the narrow-skulled *caethion*
> labour the changing shifts
> > for the cosmocrats of alien lips
> in all the fair lands
> > of the dark measures . . .[10]

The poem ends with a final question which implies an identification between the Sleeping Lord and the landscape.

> Does the land wait the sleeping lord
> > or is the wasted land
> that very lord who sleeps?[11]

Besides some of David's own poems the *Agenda* special issue also contained articles on his work by some of his old friends and admirers. Kenneth Clark wrote a piece on some of David's recent paintings and Jim Ede contributed an essay entitled 'The Visual Art of David Jones'. René Hague wrote a long article, dealing chiefly with *In Parenthesis* and *The Anathemata*. There was also an essay by Louis Bonnerot, a professor at the Sorbonne, who translated *The Anathemata* into French. Not one but two contributions came from Saunders Lewis, who was by now an important correspondent and friend to David.

A co-founder in 1925 of the Welsh Nationalist Party (later Plaid Cymru), Saunders Lewis, who was just two years older than David and also a Catholic convert, was one of the leading writers in the Welsh language in the twentieth century. He wrote poetry and plays and published a study of English influences on Welsh eighteenth-century poetry entitled *A School of Welsh Augustans*. A fervent nationalist he engaged in 1936 in a token act of arson, protesting against the building of an RAF bombing school in Wales. For this he was sent to prison and dismissed from his position as lecturer in Welsh at University College, Swansea. He subsequently made his living in journalism and farming until he was appointed a lecturer at University College, Cardiff, in 1952. David's friendship with Saunders Lewis meant that he had contact with someone who had long been at the centre of Welsh political, cultural and literary consciousness.

In his two respectful essays, Saunders Lewis stressed David's concern with the 'Matter of Wales' and his Catholic faith. He saw him as 'agonizingly an artist of his time, of this century, of war and technology and futurism and abandoned folk memory'.[12] The last article in the *Agenda* special issue was by another Welshman, Aneirin Talfan Davies, Head of Programmes for BBC Wales and also a writer and critic. This final essay stresses, and rightly, the connection between David's writing and that of the great pioneering Modernist, James Joyce.

Involvement with *Agenda* was not the only way in which David was associated with the Modernist tradition in the 1960s. Stuart Montgomery's publishing house, Fulcrum Press, another important literary venture of the decade, had, like *Agenda*, the objective of furthering the Modernist revival that began in that decade. For instance, in 1965 Fulcrum published Basil Bunting's masterpiece *Briggflatts*. And in 1967 it also published David's poem 'The Tribune's Visitation' a clear indication of his literary kinship with the resurgent Modernism, which challenged the notions of poetry and poetics associated with Philip Larkin and other anti-Modernist Movement poets who had established themselves in the 1950s. 'The Tribune's Visitation' had been broadcast on the BBC in April 1958 and printed in the *Listener* the following May. Stuart Montgomery undertook to restore it to circulation. The subject of the poem is imperialism, a theme common to many Modernist texts, such as Ezra Pound's *Homage to Sextus Propertius*, T.S. Eliot's *The Waste Land* and James Joyce's *Ulysses* to name but three. The setting of the poem is Judea and the main and central part of the poem is an address given by the Tribune, a Roman officer, to a cohort of imperial troops from Italy. Prior to his speech there are exchanges and dialogue between him, a sergeant and the men, which are often reminiscent of the language of the First World War. At times the officer's language is colloquial; at other times it is so richly intricate and rhetorical that the speech has to be regarded as a *poème en prose*, a mode of writing deriving from Baudelaire that often recurs in Modernist poetry.

The burden of the Tribune's speech is that to live in and by and for a particular locality and culture is not possible any more; it is a thing of the past. Ironically he echoes Wordsworth, a great poet of locality, when he tells the soldiers: 'I have a word to say, to say to you as men and as a man speaking to men'. What he has to tell them is that today one must live in and for the Roman world order.

It's the world-bounds

we're detailed to beat

to discipline the world-floor

to a common level

till everything presuming difference

178

and all the sweet remembered demarcations
wither
to the touch of us
and know the fact of empire.[13]

Part of the pathos of the poem is that the Tribune is still attracted to his native place and has to struggle in order to be hard-nosed and to serve the imperial standardization of the world. Clearly in one way the poem is a metaphor for the situation of all small countries and cultures – Wales, for instance. 'The Tribune's Visitation' leads us to recall David's criticisms of British imperialism in his 1930s essay on fascism. The poem also suggests that with the establishment of an imperial world order comes a movement towards secularization. The third and final section of the work, which is no longer prose but lineated as poetry, shows the Tribune administering a communion. But it is not a religious communion but rather a secular one, in which the men swear an oath *Idem in me* (the same for me) to the head of the imperial world order – Caesar.

After the publication of 'The Tribune's Visitation' David continued to work on his other Roman poems, but his progress was severly impeded when, in June 1970 at the age of seventy-four, he had a serious accident. Two days after a very slight stroke, when he was piling books on to his bed after breakfast, he fell and broke a bone in his hip. He was taken to a private ward in Harrow Hospital on Roxeth Hill where he spent several weeks. He was then moved to the Bethanie Convent in Hornsey Lane, Highgate. Unable to take care of himself properly he took refuge with the Little Sisters of Mary, the nuns of the Calvary Nursing Home on Sudbury Hill in Harrow. Here he was tended for the remaining four years of his life.

Here he had a spartan room with walls that were entirely

bare except for a single iron crucifix. But his health improved here and soon the succession of visitors, friends and admirers, who had come to see him in his previous single rooms, resumed. One of them was William Blissett, a professor of English at the University of Toronto, who had been visiting David off and on since 1959. Going to the Calvary Nursing Home for the first time in September 1970, Blissett found David looking much older than when he had last seen him, about a year before. He also showed signs of having had a stroke. There was a sagging in the facial muscles on one side and a slight slurring in his speech. On another visit, a month later, Blissett was quite shocked to see how a young nun, new to the place, treated David patronizingly and even rudely, 'as if he were a deaf infant'. Reprovingly Blissett remarked that her patient was a much honoured and respected writer and painter. David winced, Blissett was surprised to learn later that David had told no one at the nursing home that he wrote and painted. 'Here he was one of God's poor and was content to be so.'[14]

In June 1971 Blissett brought another Canadian, his student, the twenty-five-year-old Thomas Dilworth, to meet David. Dilworth's MA thesis was about David and so too was his PhD, and he was to make criticism and editing of David's work the focus of his academic career and to become a leading figure in David Jones scholarship.

In his recollection of conversations with David, Blissett indicated how David's health steadily deteriorated at this time. In August 1972 he looked unshaven, ill and in low spirits. When a kind old nursing sister tried to persuade him to go and sit in the garden on a warm summer day, he refused. Nevertheless the sister said of him, 'Such a dear, sweet man.'[15] In the last week of that month he had to be taken up to London to see a bone specialist in Harley Street. But for all his physical discomfort it was always David's

180

custom to escort his departing visitors from his room to the nursing home entrance using his recently acquired walker. When it came time to say goodbye David would give his visitor a blessing.

The following January he was horrified to experience a recurrence of his 'old nervous trouble'. 'Rosie', it seemed, had returned. Fortunately this time his doctors were able to control it quickly with new medication.

In May 1973 one of David's many visitors was his very old friend and publisher, Douglas Cleverdon, whom he had known for going on fifty years. Cleverdon, who had also been the producer of the BBC radio performance of *In Parenthesis* in 1946, now had white hair but was still extremely lively and stimulating.

Another pleasure for David at this time was the news that *Agenda* magazine was planning to honour him with a second special issue; which appeared in autumn–winter 1973/4. The issue opened with two recent poems by David. 'The Narrows', the shorter and lesser of the two, had first been published a few months earlier in *The Anglo-Welsh Review*. The then editor of that periodical, Roland Mathias, in the introduction to a corrected edition of the poem published eight years later, in 1981, has recalled how he had asked David for a poem for the fiftieth number of *The Anglo-Welsh Review*. Belatedly Mathias received 'The Narrows'. It was, David explained, the development of a 'fragment written in about 1942'. Mathias and David exchanged three versions of the poem before they had an agreed typescript. Mathias remembered how the versions would return from David 'heavily annotated in various coloured inks', accompanied by letters 'running to eighteen pages of foolscap, written downwards, sideways and roundabout'.[16] However, despite all their efforts the poem as printed in *The Anglo-Welsh Review* and *Agenda* did contain some mistakes. This is what prompted Roland Mathias to publish his corrected edition in 1981.

'The Narrows' is a dramatic monologue spoken by a Roman soldier to his fellow legionary, Porrex. He discourses on the endlessness of the wars fought by the Roman Empire and the ceaseless long marches its soldiers must engage in. He ponders the vast extent of the Empire, surveying it from the Black Sea to the Straits of Dover, the Narrows. The Kent coast is 'the Kantion shore', the adjective given to it, David told Roland Mathias, by 'a Greek of Massilia, Pythias I think, by name, a contemporary of Alexander the Great'.[17] The coast of Britain is described in what is a four-line Imagist poem, similar in style to those written by Ezra Pound in the early days of Modernism in the 1910s. (David insisted that the first word in the third line 'cliffs' be read as a verb.)

> And on the heights above the spume-fret
> the albescent chalk
> cliffs gleam-bright
> her sea-ward parapets.[18]

On the penultimate page of 'The Narrows' the speaker's remarks about Roman imperialism becomes conspicuously relevant to modern imperialisms. He sees monopoly capitalism as part of the imperialist system, and one that is going to produce still more war.

> Still more, and internecine too
> when the cosmocrats of the dark aeon
> find themselves
> wholly at a loss
> in the meandered labyrinth of
> their own monopolies.[19]

But communism is no answer. Whimsically it is mocked in the last seven lines of the poem.

> I wonder how the Dialectic
> works far-side the Styx
> or if blithe Helen toes the Party Line.[20]

The concluding two lines suggest that there will be no withering away of the state as Marxists have predicted. All that can be relied on in human life is the eternal, wearying fact of war.

The other, more intricate and less baldly assertive poem in the second special issue of *Agenda* is 'The Kensington Mass'. Its title, as René Hague suggests in his notes in *The Roman Quarry*[21], alludes to the Carmelite church in Kensington Church Street, which David attended in the early 1940s when he was lodging in nearby Sheffield Terrace and drafting the first version of the poem. The poem is reminiscent of *The Anathemata* in that it contains a sequence of free associations that come into the mind of the poet in attendance at the celebration of the Mass. The poem has an extensive dedication to Father John O'Connor, who had received David into the Roman Catholic Church at St Cuthbert's, Bradford, more than half a century before. And the first third of the work describes the actions and the sounds of the language spoken by Father O'Connor in celebrating the Mass, language that reveals both his Irish origins and his time spent in Rome. At the point in the Mass at which the priest kisses the altar cloths, the poet recalls other significant adornments: 'the chiton hem' of Helen of Troy and 'the long tunica' of the mythical Elen of Britain. Then the focus moves to Elen's infatuated husband, the Emperor, who we see setting out to hunt just before dawn in Rome. After this comes another dawn, this time in

Jerusalem, with a description of St Peter – 'the Fisherman with the Keys' – just prior to the moment the dawn cock crows for the third time.

When David allowed William Cookson to publish 'The Kensington Mass' in *Agenda*, he asked for a Note to be printed with it, stating that it was 'an unfinished draft of a poem'. It was only 'as much as he had written to date (16.2.74) in time for inclusion in this special issue'.[22] Certainly the work does not read like a unified or completed work, though there is power in its many images, for instance in this succinct characterization of Peter, the fisherman.

> His hands wide-fisted
> hands and whole frame built to
> haul and reef and steer
> His steer-tree more than most
> could manage.[23]

In that same issue of *Agenda*, the editor William Cookson praised David's poetry, including the volume *The Sleeping Lord and Other Fragments*, published by Faber in 1974, by referring to a venerable concept from Romantic poetics used by David himself.

Cookson wrote.

Much poetry today is characterized by emotion without intellect and fancy without imagination. (Ted Hughes's *Crow* is an obvious illustration of what I mean.) It is David's unique imagination which most distinguishes his work from that of his contemporaries. This esemplastic power, to use Coleridge's phrase, illuminates every page of *The Sleeping Lord and Other Fragments*, bringing unity to seemingly diverse material. It is the same quality that closely knits together both his writing and painting, which is all *one*, from his earliest drawings and from *In Parenthesis*, to his most recent poems. This singleness of texture is present in the work of most major artists, but it is, I think, more marked in David Jones than in any other poet.[24]

David will surely have been pleased by this statement of admiration. Less pleasing was his omission from *The Oxford Book of Twentieth-Century English Verse*, recently edited by Philip Larkin. A large number of people wrote to Larkin to protest, and at the Foyles literary dinner held at the Dorchester Hotel in London to launch the anthology, the Scottish poet Hugh MacDiarmid vociferously denounced the omission.

Early in 1974 David received a major honour. He received a letter from Buckingham Palace, informing him that he had been made a Companion of Honour in the birthday honours list, that is to say, that he had been admitted to the order, the membership of which was limited to sixty-six persons distinguished in the arts and in the public services. With some embarrassment he wrote to say that his health would not allow him to travel to London to receive the award from the Queen. He was very touched when a reply came from the Palace confirming that the order could be delivered to him by an equerry, and expressing much concern for his health and well-being.

A programme of readings of David's poetry at the Mermaid Theatre was organized by René Hague in the spring of 1974. It went off very well, but by now David was becoming too ill to enjoy his success. That April he was frequently unable to get out of bed, and bathing was a very difficult task which left him exhausted. He needed help in going to the lavatory and later in the year fell and hurt himself when he insisted on dispensing with such assistance. A visitor who saw him on the last day of September described him as looking 'very tired and frail'.[25] When his dinner was brought in on a tray he had considerable difficulty in lifting the food to his mouth with a knife and fork. Over the next few weeks he grew weaker and weaker and on 29 October 1974, three days before his seventy-ninth birthday, he died.

The funeral service was held at St Mary Magdalen Church in his home town of Brockley on 5 November and he was buried in the family grave in Ladywell Cemetery, Lewisham. On 13 December there was a Solemn Requiem for him in Westminster Cathedral, with many of his numerous friends attending.

David Jones died intestate but on the last day of 1974 the District Probate Registry at Brighton granted letters of administration to his sister's three children: his nieces Stella Wright and Mollie Elkin and his nephew, Anthony James Hyne.

Obituaries appeared in newspapers in the United States as well as in Britain. The *New York Times* and the *Washington Post* both remarked on his work as a writer, painter and engraver. In the latter category both newspapers singled out his 1929 series of illustrations of Coleridge's *The Rime of the Ancient Mariner* for special mention. The obituary in the *Daily Telegraph*, written by David Holloway, forthrightly and correctly identified David's achievement as a writer as greater than that as a painter: 'Although his watercolours and engravings were widely admired and exist in some quantity, his enduring fame will come from his two published books, *In Parenthesis* and *The Anathemata*.' Holloway's concluding sentence is the necessary and proper assertion: 'Because he wrote very long poems which do not break up into anthologized sections,

Jones's work has never been widely known, but it will have an assured place as part of 20th century literature.'

The obituary that appeared in *The Times* on 29 October. 1974 was a lengthy and carefully considered one, appropriately so as this had always been David's preferred newspaper, and it had published many letters from him over the years. The anonymous author – who clearly had known David – gave a detailed account of David's career and characterized his major paintings and writings. The obituarist concluded with an assessment of his personality which must surely ring true for those of us who did not know him: 'David Jones was a singularly dignified, gentle, and warm spirit, amused and amusing.'

Epilogue

PHYSICALLY DAVID JONES'S LIFE was often uncomfortable, even painful. Small and frail as a boy and a young man, he lived, after his first breakdown in his late thirties, in a continual state of anxiety that 'Rosie' might return – as indeed she did, more than once. In his adult life he also suffered from a deep-seated social malaise. In dealing with aristocrats such as Lady Chichester and Prudence Pelham and their like he lacked the confidence and aplomb exhibited by D. H. Lawrence – similarly upwardly mobile from the working class – in his relations with Lady Ottoline Morrell and the Asquiths and their friends. David once told Tom Burns in a letter that socially he was but a 'supernumerary attached, pending allocation to unit' (as the military jargon goes) to the upper classes – 'yet with my roots among the lower orders (of whom I have *great fear* and whose reactions I *hate* but for whom I feel a deep *understanding* at the same time)'.[1] René Hague also recalled David saying that among the upper classes he felt himself to be an 'impostor' but was impressed by the 'assured standing of the upper classes' which was 'based on the aristocracy of birth and tradition'.[2]

Sexually, too, David was insecure. He very much appreciated women and loved several over his lifetime, but he was never able to sustain a lasting relationship. Petra Gill, Prudence Pelham and Valerie Price all meant a great deal to him and in each case he was devastated when he lost them. One of the worst of the pains and frustrations of his life was that he was an intensely sensuous man who was not physically or sexually robust enough ever to establish himself as a lover or a husband.

Yet despite these several unhappinesses the overall impression that the story of David's life leaves is not one of miserableness. The life is redeemed by its great creativity, a creativity that shows itself in various forms. David was gifted as an essayist, a poet, a painter and an engraver. As a painter he is an important figure in the history of British art in the last century, albeit not in the first rank. For his time he was a very conservative artist, rejecting abstraction and other innovations and persevering with his delicate, highly detailed and sometimes rather scholarly manner of representational painting. But his output was large and generally of a high standard and all the more impressive coming from one who so often lacked a sense of personal well-being.

As a writer he is a major figure in twentieth-century literature and, more particularly in the Modernist tradition. *In Parenthesis* is one of Modernism's great texts. *The Anathemata* and the shorter poems, too, contain some distinguished writing. In terms of literary history he appears today as one who completes the geographical range of British Modernism in literature. Modernism emphasized the image, the particular, and specific places such as East Coker, Briggflatts, Ballylee and certain streets in Dublin. What Yeats and Joyce did with Ireland, Hugh MacDiarmid with Scotland, and T. S. Eliot and D.H. Lawrence, also treating very specific places, with England, David Jones did for Wales. By evoking certain Welsh places with all their associations he extended and changed our understanding of the meaning of 'Britain', and of the geological and historical processes that brought Britain into being.

But it is the quality of his writing, rather than the aesthetics and poetics upon which they are based, that has established him as a figure in literary history. An important part of this quality was his success in dealing, ambitiously, with profound issues of experience – redemption in its various forms, emotional, psychological and Christian, being the principal one. It is appropriate that this was a major literary theme because his writings, together with his paintings, were the way in which a life made up of much suffering was itself redeemed. David Jones's life, like his art, remains a memorable and moving testimony to the restorative powers of the human spirit.

Notes

Abbreviations used in the Notes

ANA David Jones, *The Anathemata* (London: Faber and Faber, 1952)
DG David Jones, *Dai Greatcoat: A Self-Portrait of David Jones in his Letters* ed. René Hague (London: Faber and Faber, 1980)
DYG David Jones, *The Dying Gaul and Other Writings* ed. Harman Grisewood (London: Faber and Faber, 1978)
E&A David Jones, *Epoch and Artist* (London: Faber and Faber, 1959, paperback 1973)
IP David Jones *In Parenthesis* (London: Faber and Faber, 1937, paperback 1963)
LC William Blissett, *The Long Conversation* (Oxford: O.U.P., 1981)
M&P *David Jones: Man and Poet* ed. with an introduction by John Matthias (National Poetry Foundation, Inc. University of Maine, 1989)
MU J. Miles and D. Shiel *David Jones: The Maker Unmade* (Poetry Wales Press Ltd., 1995)
RQ David Jones, *The Roman Quarry and Other Sequences* ed. Harman Grisewood and René Hague (London: Agenda Editions, 1981)
SL David Jones, *The Sleeping Lord* (London: Faber and Faber, 1974)

1 Family, Childhood and Youth 1895–1909

1. 'Welsh Culture' in *DG*, p. 118.
2. 'In Illo Tempore' in *DG*, p. 21.
3. 'Autobiographical Talk' in *E & A*, pp. 26–7.
4. *MU*, p. 13.
5. *MU*, p. 252.
6. John Warren, *St James' Parish – 150 Years of Celebration* (London: Deptford Forum Publishing, 1995).
7. *Agenda*, Vols 11–12, 1973–4, 24.
8. *DG*, p. 23.

9. 'Autobiographical Talk' in *E & A*, p. 27.
10. *ANA*, p. 41.
11. *Agenda*, Vols 11–12, 1973–4, 24.
12. 'The Tutelar of the Place' in *SL*, p. 59–60. The Welsh word 'brethyn' means 'cloth'.
13. 'In Illo Tempore', *DG*, p. 25.
14. Ibid., p. 25.
15. Ibid.
16. Ibid., p. 23.
17. Robin Ironside, *David Jones*, (Harmondsworth: Penguin, 1949), p. 4.
18. 'In Illo Tempore' in *DG*, p. 26.

2 At the Camberwell School of Art 1909–14

1. 'In Illo Tempore' in *DG*, p. 26.
2. *LC*, pp. 101–2.
3. Thomas Dilworth, *The Shape of Meaning in the Poetry of David Jones*, (Toronto: University of Toronto Press, 1988), pp. 204–5.
4. 'A Note on Mr. Berenson's Views' in *E&A* p. 273.
5. LTF no pagination.
6. *DG*, p. 60.
7. Dilworth op.cit., p. 12.
8. *Agenda*, Vols 11–12, 1973–4, 92.
9. A. S. Hartrick, *A Painter's Pilgrimage Through Fifty Years* (Cambridge: Cambridge University Press, 1939), p. 233.

3 Soldiering 1915–18

1. Letter to Saunders Lewis, 1971, in *Agenda*, Vols 11–12, 1973–4.
2. *DG*, p. 217.
3. Ibid., p. 254.
4. *IP*, pp. 6–7.
5. *ANA*, p. 216.
6. *MU*, p. 289.
7. *DG*, p. 238.
8. Ibid., p. 259.
9. Ibid., p. 174.
10. Ibid., p. 250.
11. Ibid., p. 248.
12. Ibid., p. 252.
13. Ibid., p. 29.
14. *L.C.* p. 58.
15. *DG*, p. 78.

4   The Westminster School of Art 1919–21

1. *MU*, p. 44.
2. Quoted in Robert Speaight, *The Life of Eric Gill* (London: Methuen, 1966), p. 124.
3. Jacques Maritain, *Art and Scholasticism* (London: Sheed and Ward, 1930), pp. 83–4.
4. Walter Bayes in 'The Grammar of Drawing' Pt 1 in the *Architectural Review* (London, January 1924), 12.
5. *E & A*, p. 171–2.
6. *LC*, p. 129.
7. *DG*, p. 170.

5   Eric Gill and Ditchling Common 1921–4

1. Fiona MacCarthy, *Eric Gill* (London and Boston: Faber and Faber, 1989), p. 143.
2. Robert Speaight, *The Life of Eric Gill* (London: Methuen, 1966), p. 111.
3. *M & P*, p. 96.
4. Quoted in *MU*, p. 42.
5. Ibid.
6. Quoted in Jonathan Miles *Eric Gill and David Jones at Capel-y-ffin* (Bridgend: Seren Books, 1992), p. 24.

6   Wales and France 1924–8

1. Barbara Wall, *René Hague A Personal Memoir* (The Aylesford Press, 1989), p. 26.
2. Merlin James, *David Jones 1895–1974. A Map of the Artist's Mind* (London: Lund Humphries, 1995), p. 14.
3. Jonathan Miles, *Eric Gill and David Jones at Capel-y-ffin* (Bridgend: Seren Books, 1992), pp. 135–6.
4. *DG*, p. 17.
5. Ibid., p. 33.
6. Ibid., p. 34.
7. Quoted in *MU*, p. 152.
8. Ibid., p. 152.
9. Ibid., p. 151.
10. Ibid., p. 152.
11. *DYG*, p. 187.
12. Eric Gill, *Autobiography* (London: Jonathan Cape, 1940), p. 230.
13. Nicolete Gray, *The Paintings of David Jones* (London: Gordon Fraser, 1981), p. 25.
14. *DG*, pp. 45–6.
15. *MU*, p. 110.

16. *DYG*, p. 29.
17. Ibid.

7   Years of Attainment 1928–32

1. Harman Grisewood in conversation, 31 October 1992. Quoted in *MU* p. 158.
2. Tom Burns, *The Use of Memory* (London: Sheed and Ward, 1993), p. 164.
3. 'Helen Sutherland', unpublished memoir, cited in *MU*, pp. 173–4.
4. Letter to René Hague, 7 May 1966 in NLW.

8   Depression Years 1932–6

1. William Blissett *The Long Conversation: A Memoir of David Jones* (Oxford: OUP, 1981), p. 67.
2. *DG*, p. 55.
3. *MU*, p. 138–9.
4. Tom Burns, *The Use of Memory* (London: Sheed and Ward, 1993), p. 165.
5. *M & P*, p. 102.
6. Ibid.
7. *LC*, p. 84.
8. Thomas Hodgkin, *Letters from Palestine 1932–6* (London: Quartet Books, 1986), p. 64.
9. Ibid., p. 60.
10. *MU*, p. 103.
11. Burns, op. cit., p. 164.
12. Ibid.
13. Prudence Pelham, letter to David Jones, October and November 1937, quoted in *MU*, p. 180.
14. Cited in *MU*, p. 163.
15. David Jones, 'Letter to H. S. Ede', in John Matthias (ed.) *M & P*, p. 112.
16. *M & P*, p. 198.

9   *In Parenthesis* 1937

1. 'A Dream of John Ball' in *Three Works by William Morris*, (London: Lawrence and Wishart, 1968), p. 54.
2. Ibid., p. 51.
3. *In Parenthesis*, p. 127.
4. Ibid., p. 138.
5. Ibid., p. 108.
6. Ibid., p. 162.
7. Ibid., p. 176.
8. Ibid., p. 163.

10   The Attractions of Adolf Hitler 1937–9

1. *DG*, p. 82.
2. Jones letter to H. S. Ede of 25 November 1936 in Kettle's Yard, Cambridge, quoted in *MU*, p. 179.
3. *LC*, p. 66.
4. Barbara Wall, *René Hague A Personal Memoir* (Wirral: The Aylesford Press, 1989), p. 26.
5. *MU*, p. 163.
6. Quoted in *MU*, p. 175.
7. Tom Burns, *The Use of Memory* (London: Sheed and Ward, 1993), pp. 165–6.
8. *M & P*, p. 152.
9. Ibid., p. 148.
10. Ibid., p. 150.
11. Ibid., p. 151.
12. Ibid., p. 156.
13. *DG*, p. 104.
14. *DG*, p. 100.
15. *RQ*, p. 197.
16. Ibid., p. 193.
17. Ibid., p. 189.
18. Ibid.
19. Ibid., p. 204.
20. Ibid., p. 211.
21. Ibid., p. XXIV.
22. *ANA*, p. 32.
23. *RQ*, p. 95.
24. Ibid., p. 24.
25. Ibid., p. 121.
26. Ibid., p. 127.

11   The War Years 1939–45

1. *E & A*, p. 299.
2. Ibid., pp. 300–01.
3. *M & P*, p. 115.
4. Ibid., p. 114.
5. Ibid., p. 115.
6. *E & A*, p. 221.
7. Ibid., p. 240.
8. Ibid., p. 241.
9. Ibid., p. 250.
10. *DG*, p. 134.
11. Ibid., p. 150.
12. Ibid., p. 161.
13. *M & P*, p. 116.

14. *MU*, p. 283.
15. *LC*, p. 121.
16. Ibid., p. 105.

12   Illness and Achievement 1946–52

1. *M & P*, p. 116.
2. Ibid.
3. Quoted in *MU*, p. 190.
4. Ibid.
5. Ibid., p. 192, Tate Gallery Archive.
6. *M & P*, p. 108.
7. *MU*, p. 40.
8. *DG*, p. 150.
9. *MU*, p. 201.
10. 'A Note on Mr. Berenson's Views' in *E & A*, p. 276.
11. 'James Joyce's Dublin', in *E & A*, p. 304.
12. Ibid., pp. 306–7.
13. 'The Heritage of Early Britain' in *E & A*, p. 197.
14. Ibid., p. 199.
15. 'The Arthurian Legend', in *E & A*, p. 204.
16. Ibid., p. 209.
17. Ibid., p. 211.
18. *M & P*, p. 118.
19. *ANA* (1972 edition), p. 131.
20. Ibid., p. 80.
21. René Hague, *A Commentary on The Anathemata of David Jones*, University of Toronto, 1977, p. 112.
22. *ANA* (1972 edn), p. 170.
23. Ibid., p. 120.
24. Hague, *A Commentary* op. cit., p. 155.
25. *ANA* (1972 edn), p. 168.
26. Ibid., p. 170.
27. Ibid., p. 173.
28. Ibid., p. 237.
29. Ibid., p. 243.
30. Ibid., p. 95.

13   Years of Honour 1953–64

1. *E & A*, pp. 47–8.
2. 'Changes in the Coronation Service' in *E & A*, p. 49.
3. Ibid., p. 50.
4. 'The Wall', in *SL*, p. 14.
5. Ibid.
6. *Letters to William Hayward*, (London: Agenda Editions, 1979), p. 76.
7. *MU*, p. 271.
8. *DG*, p. 177.

9. *DYG*, p. 17.
10. 'The Tutelar of the Place' in *SL*, p. 61.
11. Ibid., p. 62.
12. Ibid., pp. 62–3.
13. *MU*, p. 226.
14. *MU*, p. 161.
15. Ibid., p. 192.
16. *M & P*, p. 53.
17. Ibid.
18. *Letters to William Hayward*, op. cit., pp. 75–6.
19. *M & P*, p. 67.
20. 'The Fatigue' in *SL*, pp. 31–2.

14   The Last Decade 1964–74

1. David Jones, *Letters to Vernon Watkins* (Cardiff: University of Wales Press, 1976), p. 11.
2. Ibid., p. 77.
3. *DG*, p. 210.
4. *LC*, p. 70.
5. *MU*, p. 161, Letter to Dorothea de Halpert of 29 December 1960, in the possession of Beatrix Dufort.
6. *SL*, p. 69.
7. Ibid., p. 67.
8. Ibid., p. 9.
9. Ibid., pp. 76–7.
10. Ibid., pp. 90–91.
11. Ibid., p. 96.
12. Saunders Lewis, *Agenda*, Vol. 5, Nos.1–3, Spring–Summer 1967, p. 112.
13. *RQ*, p. 53.
14. *LC*, p. 67.
15. Ibid., p. 97.
16. Roland Mathias, Introduction to David Jones, *The Narrows*, (Budleigh Salterton, Devon: Intcrim Prcss, 1981), no pagination.
17. Ibid.
18. Ibid.
19. Ibid.
20. Ibid.
21. *RQ*, p. 233.
22. *Agenda*, Vol. 12 No. 1 Autumn–Winter 1973–74, p. 11.
23. Ibid., p. 10.
24. Ibid., p. 31.
25. *LC*, p. 146.

Epilogue

1. *DG*, p. 107.
2. *DG*, p. 136.

Index